The Pro

MW01678175

Jana's fluenc... ...omplex and often "taboo" subject of death is remarkable. I plunged in this book and found Jana's passion about the dual subjects of life and death to be enriching, comforting, and educational—her wonderful perspective, interspersed with so many meaningful stories, adds dimension and heart to this book. I know from my own experience that this kind of book is filled with information that people will love to be able to find when they need it.

—Mary R. Truscott, author of
Brats: Children of the American Military Speak Out

I read the book straight through in one sitting. It articulates the universal experience of life and death and the connection between them....Though we cannot rationalize the death experience, Jana's book depicts the journey and the gifts the death experience begets. The polarities of life and death provide insight to living a full and glorious life despite its limitations. A must read!

—Rory LaBahn, Elementary School Teacher

Jana provides a very realistic and personal view of death while graciously offering each reader a riveting fervor to live each day with sincerity and zest.

—Franz Freibert, Ph.D. Scientist

Additional Praise for
The Promise of Death, the Passion of Life

Jana, you have a very positive energy around you and it is felt by those you come in contact with. Your book can help many people treasure relationships and the memories that they have made and continue to make throughout their lives. Thank you for sharing some of your life experiences with us.

—Rebecca Stedry, Hospital Gift Shop Manager

The first person accounts in this book have helped me as well as the clients I serve better tie together an enhanced authentic daily living through the experience of death. I have come to the conclusion through Jana's writing how important it is to understand that no one gets out of here alive, thus we should live fully every moment. What a pleasure to read this book.

—Mark Boshelli, M.S., LPCC, Clinical Director for Community Mental Health Centers

The Promise of Death, The Passion of Life

A Reflective Exploration of Death, Loss, and Living Fully

JANA BALDRIDGE VARGAS

Rancho Cucamonga, California

To contact the author or to order more books, please visit:
www.thepromiseandthepassion.com

Original cover art by Elias Vargas
To see more of Elias' work, please visit www.eliasvargas.com

Back cover photo by Robert Garcia

Published by Luminary Enterprises, Inc.
P.O. Box 877
Rancho Cucamonga, CA 91729

Publisher's Cataloguing-in-Publication Data
Vargas, Jana Baldridge.

The promise of death, the passion of life : a reflective exploration of death, loss, and living fully / Jana Baldridge Vargas. – Rancho Cucamonga, CA : Luminary Enterprises, Inc., 2005.

p. ; cm.
ISBN: 0-9771763-0-4
ISBN13: 978-0-9771763-0-4

1. Death—Psychological aspects. 2. Grief—Psychological aspects. 3. Loss (Psychology) I. Title.

BF789.D4 V37 2005
155.9/37—dc22 2005931348

Book production and coordination by Jenkins Group, Inc.
www.bookpublishing.com
Interior design: Debbie Sidman
Cover design: Jana Baldridge Vargas

Printed in the United States of America.
09 08 07 06 05 • 5 4 3 2 1

For my Lee,
with whom all things are possible.

Contents

Acknowledgments

Like most authors, I would like to thank many wonderful people without whom this book could not have happened. Some are aware of their impact on my life and my writing, some are not. This space allows me the opportunity to publicly proclaim their importance in my life, their relevance to my journey, their contribution to the work in progress that is me.

First to my parents Chuck and Jane Baldridge, you were my first teachers, thank you for the first lesson on death and the countless others that followed. Thank you for helping me to see that learning never ends. To my children, Elias and Hilary Vargas, thank you for routing your journeys through me. You have taught me far more than I will ever teach you. To my sister, Allison Baldridge Hoskins, my first friend, growing up with you was wonderful—growing older with you is even better. To my treasured friend, Marcie Davis, thank you for allowing me to share part of your story, and even more so thank you for your unwavering support and guidance, your love and friendship. To my enduring friend, Carol Hart, thank you for the many years of love and closeness despite distance and thank you for allowing me to share the lesson of your challenge and your confrontation with it. To my cherished friend, Kim Lawrence, you are one of my heroes. To Joanne Dodson, thank you for sharing with me your bravery in the face of loss, your fierce love and commitment to your man. To a professor of the profound, Bernard McGrane, your support and encouragement have stayed with me years beyond school and will stay with me always. Finally, I hold a heart full of love and gratitude for Carla Olson, my soul sister, my kindred spirit—my Muse.

Introduction

Promise (prom'is) *n.* **1**. A declaration that something will or will not be done, given, etc by one : pledge. **2.** an express assurance on which expectation is to be based. **3.** something that has the effect of an express assurance; indication of what may be expected.

Passion (pash'en) n. 1. any powerful or compelling emotion or feeling. 2. strong amorous feeling or desire, love. 3. strong sexual desire or lust. 4. a strong or extravagant fondness, enthusiasm or desire for anything. 5. an outburst of strong emotion or feeling.

The words used for my title, passion and promise, are not chosen lightly. They are the foundation of what I believe about death and about life, that is why I have bothered to define them above. I want us all to be very clear about what these words mean to me and why I am using them. When I say you are promised death and loss, I am not trying to instill fear, quite the opposite. I am saying that it is simply an assurance, it can and should be expected. When I write about living passionately I am not talking about the kind of love passion we find in romance novels or in the movies, although at times you can have that kind of love. I am talking about living your life with powerful and compelling emotion. I am talking about a life lived with strong enthusiasm and about approaching all of the moments of your life with care and deep feeling.

No matter what your spiritual inclinations are, or what religion you follow, or whether you consider yourself a believer at all, no matter your political affiliations, or lack thereof, no matter your education, occupation, or avocation, no matter your culture, national origin, skin color or ethnic identity, no matter your sexual orientation, marital status or gender, we all have one great thing in common—every single person we know, every single person we love, is going to die and so are we. The only question is will it happen to you before it happens to them. Our own death is something we will face once, but facing loss is something we will do over and over in our lifetimes. Unless you die first, you will face loss, lots of it. While some of us may escape the enormity of some losses, such as the loss of a child, and some of us may seem to have a far greater amount of loss than the next person, and still others of us may die before we have had much loss—loss is inevitable. Death is inescapable.

Death is the only thing we are promised at birth, it is the only thing we can expect—*for sure* and not just for ourselves. Death awaits everyone we know and love. So what can we do about that, if anything? What can we possibly do besides hide ourselves in caves isolated from others in order to avoid attachment in the first place? How do we go forward? How do we, once we accept this is a certainty, dare to expose ourselves to love and its inevitable loss? How can we face the very thing that brings us such pain and fear? How can we keep death at the forefront of our thoughts and decisions when the very mention of it sends chills down our spines and strikes terror into our hearts?

In this book, I would like to explore some self-evident truths about life and its inherent losses, I would like to share some personal experiences with loss and with life. Each of us has our own journey to make, these are ours to decide what to do with, but by sharing journeys we can find meaning for our own path. We can find in our heart what is the right way for our lives. My journey has led me to a place where I know we can use death as a tool to embrace life more fully. On my journey, it is the experiences with death and loss that have shaped and defined my life and have led to a more passionate and rich existence.

In Aldous Huxley's horrific tale of life in the future, *Brave New World*, he depicts a time in which people are not born to mothers and families, when their life's work is predetermined and their emotions managed and controlled. In this terrifying tale, it is revealed throughout the story that the controllers felt the need to diminish passion in order to better serve what they felt to be the societal good. They explain that in order to control passion they had to eliminate the contemplation of death, the reflection of life's impermanence. In this tale of a controlled society driven to consume without question, to work without thought people, through conditioning and medication, are completely blasé about death. For them death is irrelevant and therefore they no longer have the messy reality of passion, passion that causes the extreme and individualistic behavior that this futuristic world cannot abide. Though this timeless tale of a society gone too far holds many lessons, one of the most significant to me is that it is clear you need one to have the other, passion and death are interlinked. One cannot exist without the other. It was the reality of death that had to be softened in order that passion would no longer prevail.

The reality of death is harsh, there is no shielding that, but that does not mean we cannot embrace the truth of death. We don't have to run away in fear or shrink back from this perfectly normal and predictable part of life. Why fear the one thing we know? We don't have to like it, and we won't, but we can find ways to live passionately with the promise of death. The promise of death is in fact the key to the passion of life, to the intensity of living now, aware of this promise. The passion of life and the promise of death are in fact the flip sides of the same coin. You will see that if you embrace one you are already embracing the other. Life is precious and it is death that makes it so.

CHAPTER 1

Death Experiences

Everyone has a history of death and loss experiences of their own. If you are reading this book, loss has happened to you. Whether you realize it or not, these experiences have shaped who you are and how you react, how you face challenge and pain. Preparing for and acknowledging the force of death and loss in our lives should be one of the foremost aspects of our existence. For what is life, but a road to death? This does not have to be a morbid thought however. Death is simply what we can expect. It is the one thing we know that is true and real in our lives. This thought has consumed writers and philosophers for thousands of years, indeed it has probably weighed on most everyone's minds from time immemorial.

In the 1500s Montaigne wrote that to philosophize is to learn to die, that we should think of nothing as often as we think of death. His view was particularly goal oriented, his belief being that the awareness of our doom should stir us to accomplish as much as possible in our short time here on earth. I would like to put a different spin on that however. I too believe we should think of nothing as often as we think of death, but not as a means to accomplish things, as a means to enjoy the beauty of life here and now, a means to love fully and to live passionately.

While Montaigne wrote with concern over his own death, for me the thing to prepare for is not our own death, but the deaths of those we love. It is good to consider that you will die, but consider too how different we can be with others when we know they are dying as well. Our own death will occur to us just once, but loss will hit us over and over and over, and it will hurt. Death is the reminder of the fragility of each moment, the significance of every tiny thing that we do. Death experiences will be the most powerful and potent times in our lives, sad and horrible yes, but opportunities to grow and open ourselves fully to love, to life and its riches.

For me, the first major loss was a wonderful dog, named Nugget. He was eight, I was eleven, my sisters ten and eight. He was our brother, our friend, our beautiful guardian and constant companion. His sudden death hit very hard and we cried and cried as only three little girls can. Compounding this horrible loss was the fact that his death was deliberate. He and three other wonderful neighborhood dogs had been poisoned by a neighbor. While my memories are softened by time, what I remember most was my father telling us, through his own tears and anguish that this was one of the things our pets teach us—we learn through them about death and loss. Our parents did not try to redirect us with a new dog. They shielded us somewhat from their own anger over this murder, but they simply allowed us our grief, our pain. They gave us room to heal on our own while they loved us through it all. I did not realize until much later how valuable their early modeling would be to me.

Though we dealt with the loss of pets in our family in a very straight forward manner, do not think for one moment that pets were not treasured in our home, they were. Like all of us, we learned far more than how to deal with loss through sharing our lives with pets. We learned unconditional love, both given and received. We learned to treasure the unique nature of each being, to revel in their little idiosyncrasies, and to celebrate their simple way of living and loving. Each pet had their own Christmas stocking, each was an integral part of the family and each was treasured and adored. Each time there was the death of a pet, there was crying, but there was healing too. I was very fortunate to have been raised by loving parents who stayed married until death did them part. We were a very close little nuclear family with two grandmothers, never having known our grandfathers. We faced very little loss via death while growing up. Through what loss we did face, we learned that life does go on and that the memories of those we have loved never leave us.

My first realization that death experiences can be life altering came when I was twenty-five years old and eight months pregnant with my second child. My husband's Aunt Aurora had become like a second mother to me as mine had moved away from my location. I would call Aurora to ask how to cook something, she would babysit our little boy once in a while, she often shared the treats from her kitchen and garden with us, we were welcome in their home at any time. My husband, Lee, just adored this particular aunt and uncle and I did too. Aurora and her husband, Tim, had accepted me into the family before I had even met Lee's parents. They clearly loved my Lee and seemed to respect his choice in me, always making me feel a part of the family. We had decided to ask them to be the godparents of our second child, though we had not done so yet.

Aurora had lymphoma, which she had had for several years but which had been in remission. I had not even been aware she had it, or had ever had it, as she was very active and healthy. It was simply never talked about. From my perspective, which was of course limited, it seemed she was just suddenly very sick. Even when sick, Aurora was always in good spirits about everything when around me and was really very accepting of illness and its consequences. I was soon to learn just how accepting she was. Aurora gave me one of the most powerful lessons I will ever receive, a gift, a life changing experience that has shaped the direction and choices in my life from then on.

As Aurora's lymphoma progressed, she began to experience large tumors appearing virtually over night. She would one day have a huge growth on her neck or elsewhere, of course these growths were occurring on the inside as well. At one point one growth seemed to have affected Aurora's ability to use one arm and it hung limply at her side. I remember taking her for a radiation treatment once and she was completely nonchalant about this arm thing. It seemed to be little more than an inconvenience for her. Aurora spoke rather freely about the cancer and said she had only asked God to allow her to raise her children when she had been initially diagnosed, and that He had granted her that.

At one point in the early fall, one of Aurora's doctors broke down when he told her she would not survive this cancer, probably not survive until Thanksgiving. She did not cry or react much at all which led the doctor to think she did not understand the gravity of what he had said.

When he asked her if she understood what he was telling her, she very casually said to him, "That's what we're born for, to die."

She comforted him, I am certain, with her peace and acceptance of such a fate. Aurora was only fifty-six years old.

My pregnancy progressed, as did Aurora's decline and one day in my eighth month I offered to help her daughters who had moved home to be nearer to her and their father as they went through this difficult time. I arranged to take a day off of work, took our little guy to his sitter's for the day and went over to help change bedding, to be with her so that they could run errands, what ever was needed. Aurora was completely bed ridden at this point and a hospice nurse was coming a few times a week, they had pain medication available as needed. We certainly knew Aurora was dying but I could not have known it would be that very day.

Throughout the day Aurora slept and waked and while she was in pain, she was given medication whenever needed and she was at peace about her circumstances. We all took turns being in her room with her, tending to anything she needed. Her husband and daughters took some time to run errands and to visit the funeral home to prepare for what was coming. While I was tending to her and visiting with her while they were out, I laid across her king-sized bed on my big, pregnant tummy. I rubbed lotion on her hands, which she loved.

Aurora apologized to me saying, "I'm sorry, this must be so hard on you."

I started to cry, telling her no, it was not hard on me, I was where I wanted to be, saying, "It must be hard on you."

She calmly told me it was not hard at all, she was ready to die, she would get to see her Patricia, her first-born who had died in childhood. Aurora comforted me and showed me such grace and calm. She had a totally fearless response to what was happening, and her sense of peace was infectious to me.

I was constantly reminded of the very unique position I found myself in, holding the hand of a dying woman while a baby wiggled fiercely inside me as I lay across my belly. I was in direct contact with life and death simultaneously and Aurora knew it. I told her we had wanted to ask her and Uncle Tim to be our baby's godparents, Aurora calmly told me that she would not make it that long. I said then if that were the case I would ask Tim and their daughter to baptize the baby and if it was a girl I would name her for Aurora. She liked that idea and then told me very directly that I was having a girl and that she had seen her. Though we had chosen not to know the sex of the baby through medical means, I knew now this was true. There was no doubt in my mind as to what Aurora knew and had seen.

Aurora was very at peace, truly coming and going throughout the day. A priest came over to the house to see her, offering her last rites but she declined saying it would be too hard on her family, would he just do a prayer for the sick instead, which he did. Toward the end of day I called my husband and said I thought it was much closer than we had realized and he had best come see her tonight. Lee picked up our four-year old son, Elias, from the sitter, dropped him with my sister Allie, and came right over. He spent an hour or so privately with Aurora, the time for goodbyes was yet another gift from this wonderful woman.

Late into the evening, we left Aurora to her family, crying our way home, stopping to pick up our boy. My sister met us with concern for Aurora and took me aside to say she had told Elias she was sorry his Aunt Aurora was so sick.

Elias had stopped his coloring to say, "I know, Jesus is coming to get her tonight."

Allie said she had chills run down her as she said to him, "Oh, Elias, I know Aurora is very sick, but honey we don't know when Jesus is coming."

He replied calmly, "*I* do, He is coming tonight."

Never underestimate how aware children are, how closely connected they can be to matters of spirit.

About an hour after we got home, after getting our boy to bed, Aurora's daughter called us to tell us her mother had just died. We called a sitter over once again and went straight to their house. We were able to be there with Aurora and her family for over four hours before the coroner's office came for the body. We cried, we held one another, we held Aurora, we did what families do at these times. I was so grateful to fate that I had spent more than eight hours that day with this family, with Aurora, that I had been witness to a passing as remarkable as this. One month later, almost to the day, our beautiful Hilary Aurora was born.

This death shaped forever how I would face death and loss. This experience with life and death juxtaposed in such an intimate and personal way was a powerful force in shaping the path of my life and the choices I would later make. We may not know at the time, but events such as these change fundamentally who we are and alter our courses in subtle and sometimes not so subtle ways. Aurora's calm acceptance was a model to me. There was no doubt at all that death held no fear for her. Her life had been full and rewarding, she was at peace—no matter her age.

I knew I would strive to emulate Aurora's peace, that acceptance of life's ultimate destination, for me that was the only way to die—face on. How to do it? That is the question. Even more so, how to face loss head on? How to accept the deaths of others? It is one thing to understand and accept one's own death, it is another to accept that you will have to accept the deaths of others, others that you love, that you cherish, that you are sure you cannot live without.

Death did not touch me again for a few years and then it was an eighty six year old grandmother. I loved her, of course, and mourned her passing, but one does expect the loss of people who are at such advanced ages.

Even as I write this, however, I am reminded that when my other grandmother died at the age of 103 several years later that very shortly before her death she had told my mother, "If I should die early, be sure you get these pictures for safe keeping."

My mom thought, "Early in the morning?"

I mean after all at 103 we're pretty much past early, but hey life's not over 'til it's over.

Perhaps the most widely read and definitive tale about the transformative power of loss and death came to us in Mitch Albom's *Tuesdays with Morrie*, his moving and passionate story about the death of his mentor and friend. This touching, heartfelt and deeply personal book reached millions of readers, resonating in a way few stories can. If you have not yet read this book, you must. I believe one of the reasons this book was so widely received was that we all long for a Morrie in our lives. We wish fervently for someone who can demonstrate to us the power of living fully and dying gracefully, one who can guide and direct us toward the loss of fear and to the embrace of love. Fortunately for us, Mitch Albom's strength and skills as a writer gave us all that Morrie, a gentle, wise man whose strength and passion for life transformed Mitch Albom further into a gentle, wise man as well. I am certain that Morrie saw all along the seeds of such compassion and strength in Mitch, but those seeds were watered into fruition when Mitch opened himself up to the lessons Morrie still had for him and for all of us.

While Mitch had his Morrie and I had my Aurora, we can and do use all of our experiences to learn and grow, whether we are involved in it, or aware of it, or not. Some deaths that have touched me have been sudden and unexpected, some have followed long illnesses where we all knew the outcome, some followed illnesses where only some of us knew the outcome. One thing is certain, losses have continued year after year, some hurt more than others, some hurt so much you hardly believe your heart can still beat. So, what can we learn from losses?

As we proceed through this text we will examine several lessons death can bring to us, from dealing with life's pain, to living life fully and completely. Consider reflection on death experiences and death in general your most available aid in living life to the fullest. There is no question that death first and foremost reminds us that life is temporary, that moments count and each one is fleeting. Reflection on death experiences will always bring us to the realization that it is the small, simple moments that mattered most. It is the time we have given those we have loved, the words we have spoken, or not, that ring over and over in our minds.

Through loss we can learn to better express ourselves with care and forethought. In reflecting on death and loss we can come to realize that it is within us to impact the grief we will inevitably feel in our lives. We will know that we must not add to our grief by allowing ourselves to suffer the pain of unexpressed emotions or words spoken harshly. How different would our grief be if every time we spoke to those we love, we remembered that they will die. With death ever present in our minds, anger and frustration can be muted considerably, how we speak to others is softened. With the inevitability of loss a conscious presence for us, we will not miss the opportunity to be good to others, to make time for others, to express our love to others. We cannot allow the words we have spoken and those we have not spoken to multiply the pain we will feel at loss, this is the part of loss that is in our hands. How do we keep such a painful reality at the forefront of our minds without dwelling constantly on the sadness of death, without becoming morbid in our preoccupation with death and loss?

Death reflection need not be a morbid experience, in fact it can be very enlightening. In reflecting on death and its lessons, we can recognize that much of our dynamics are wasted and unnecessary, we can realize more clearly what really matters at the end of the day—at the end of a life. Death makes things really simple. It causes us to reflect on all of our actions, words, and behaviors.

We all have differing views on matters of spirit and the afterlife, or whether there is an afterlife. That is not what this book is about. This book is about death, that is true, but more so it is about life, about choices we make that affect the quality of our lives. Life boils down to that—choices. The only part we have no choice about is that we must die, the rest is up to us. We can consider what it is we really need in this life, what emotions do we need to hold onto, what type of energy do we wish to send out into the world. Death reflection makes this really simple, it boils life down to its essence. As we move forward, you will see that death itself is not something to be feared, but a promise to be embraced.

CHAPTER 2

There's Pain in Life, Deal With It

For as long as I can remember I have told my kids, "There's pain in life, deal with it"—often much to their exasperation.

I am a perfectly nurturant mother, loving, and affectionate but I have never had much appreciation for whining. Even when they were little and small crises became big to them I would ultimately resort to my favorite phrase—"There's pain in life, deal with it." I felt then, and I do now, that they would ultimately need to rely on their own source of strength. My husband and I could provide the finest examples possible, we could demonstrate strength in the face of adversity and pain, we could sow in them the seeds of such strength, but they would in the end need to know it was within them to cope. I knew that over-coddling was going to be no help to them, they had to learn to face disappointment, change, challenge, and pain, physical and otherwise.

Ultimately, your children will pretty much model your behavior, you have to "get it" first, then you have to show how it's done, but you cannot do it for them. This is true about all learning, not just living with loss. We model responsible behavior, we model anger or the management of anger, we model love and compassion toward others and other living things, we model hate and prejudice, we model relationships, work ethics, humor, you name it—the kids are watching.

My kids are grown now, well on their own journeys and living full and rich lives, still linked very closely to us, but independent financially and otherwise. We have shielded them from very little, certainly not from pain, not from grief, not from harsh realities and not from death. We never spoke in euphemisms about anything as serious as death, we felt they had to know—because you never know.

One of my acquaintances told me how when ever she was driving with her kids and saw a pet dead at the side of the road she would say, "Oh, that kitty shouldn't be sleeping there, he could get hurt."

I thought "Ahhhhh!! What is she doing to them?!"

At what point will the truth be revealed? And it will be revealed. At what price does that little deception take place? It's not like Santa Claus and the Easter Bunny, which they do begin to reason out for themselves. It's not as if when they finally ask you to verify what they are suspecting, that you are Santa, you can say then, "oh, yeah, you know that sleeping kitty thing, let me tell you about death."

When is the time going to come, when you have to tell them Grandpa's nap is going to take a really long time? I don't mean to be crass here, but you are always better being honest with kids, answer only what they ask, but answer them honestly. Remember, it is all right to tell them "I don't know" sometimes too. Truthfully, there are going to be many questions you really don't have the answers to.

My reaction to dead animals at the side of the road has always been quite different from that of my acquaintance. I have a silent moment of sorrow for the path of humanity crossing their path, they simply do not stand a chance against a car. I send out a quick wish for their peace and a vocal apology, whether there are kids in my car or not, this is just what I do. I recall one day when my kids came running in the door because a neighbor's dachshund had been hit by a car at the end of our street. I had lamented this possibility for at least a year as the dog ran free, often walking right into our house. She was a precious little thing, so friendly and quiet. We always welcomed her, but I worried this was bound to happen. How could a driver possibly see a dog so low to the ground? Sure enough, it had happened.

I raced up the hill to the street where she was lying. The poor man who had hit her was crying, anguished to be the cause of her distress. Sadly, the parents of the family were not there, the teenage kids were the ones forced to respond and they were hysterical. I bent down to her and saw the blood coming from her mouth, her labored breathing, was certain her chest had been crushed, but she was awake and breathing fitfully. I sent her kids to their house to get a tray to slide her on to. She would have to get to the vet immediately, though I felt she could not survive. I gently placed my hand on her and whispered softly to her to let go, that it would be all right and I would stay with her. She slowly stopped breathing, though her eyes remained open. My kids, about 6 and 10 at the time, stood right there watching.

We slid her onto the tray, her kids unaware of her true state, and they rushed her to the vet where I knew they would at least feel they had done all they could by getting her there. I called the vet about half an hour later and confirmed what I knew, she had been dead when she arrived. I never talked to her family about this, I really didn't know them, but I know I did what I could for her passage. My kids and I talked openly about this preventable tragedy, we talked about responsibility in letting such a little thing out to run the streets like that, but I emphasized that it was much more important to focus on her passage than any blame with the family. It was sad, we cried, but it was life—these things do happen. We learned from it and life went on.

While this little dog's death was preventable at that time, it was not preventable forever. We must remember that all life dies. It is certainly appropriate and commendable to work for life promoting, life preserving measures. Causes like Mothers Against Drunk Driving, advocacy and consumer safety groups and a whole host of organizations around various life ending illnesses provide needed focus and attention to forestalling death and the alleviation of suffering. It is wonderful to see people organized around causes that seek to relieve suffering, but it does not ultimately change the reality of death. We must always remember that death will still happen eventually, pain will still happen, loss will still happen—it is simply our nature.

We all know people who use the phrase, "It's not fair." We often hear this phrase used when someone is talking about a hardship or struggle, a death or an illness. I always wonder who told them life was fair? I mean really, what would be fair? For someone else to be faced with the pain, for there never to be pain? It is just not realistic. Life is not fair.

Fair is a human construct. Fair, being impartial or just, may or may not apply to our dealings with others though if it is an attribute we favor we should surely seek to be fair in our communications and interactions with others. We hope to find fairness and justice in legal matters, but we all know how these matters really play out. The concept of fairness is an attempt at best to impose upon society some semblance of equality of rights and a common adherence to an accepted set of rules.

Don't misunderstand, I am not knocking fairness. It is a commendable effort to try to live gently with others, to live in a more harmonious fashion and peaceful existence, to better our time while here. What I am saying is that "fair" does not apply to life in general, certainly not to nature, and definitely not to death. The only thing fair about death is that we all die—no one gets to pass on that option. There will be pain in our lives and we had best deal with it.

While the death passages of those you love will certainly be among the hardest pains you will have to deal with, there are plenty of other hardships and pains as well. Stress, anxiety, changes—both good and bad, divorce, moving, failures, disappointments—these things will occur over and over in your life and you had better deal with the pain or the pain will deal with you. Do not catch yourself up in the argument about these travails not being fair, lose that idea right now and recognize that life is not fair, and deal with it.

If you do not deal with your pain, you know it will find a way to deal with you. We know that stress and unresolved inner pain leads to eating disorders, alcohol and substance abuse, dysfunctional relationships and a myriad of pains we need not endure. There are a host of books on these subjects and if you struggle with your pain or find yourself in relationships and situations that worsen your pain, you should seek ways to ameliorate it. Books, support groups, counselors, and therapists can all help lead you to where you want to go, but remember you are the one making the trip, you are the driver—the answers will be found in you.

When I say there is pain in life, deal with it, I am not suggesting that we should not feel pain, we must. Pain is an unavoidable part of life. But deal with it means just that, take the pain, experience the pain, do what you can to relieve the pain in healthy and constructive ways, but let it go when you must go forward. The pain will be there to be revisited if you need that, but I do believe if we strive to live in the present moment, which is really all we have, we can find we don't need to revisit old pain so often.

In dealing with our pain effectively and constructively, we can find ever-increasing strength within ourselves. We will find that the greater our strength in the face of challenge, adversity and pain, the greater our passion is in moments of joy. When we use the ultimate pain—the immeasurable pain of loss through death—as the learning tool it is, we can find ourselves better able to cope with those lesser pains. When we constantly remind ourselves of the temporary nature of every situation—because life is temporary—we can decrease the significance of the lesser pains. We all know when in the midst of what seems to be a crisis, if a death occurs it takes precedence. Suddenly, we can clear the calendar to be with people. Suddenly, we are not as important as we have been caught up in believing we are. Why not then try to harness this sense of significance and importance that death and loss represent to put into proper perspective life's other travails? When we keep death as our companion, as our constant reminder that all of life is temporary, we can have an ongoing sense that this too, shall pass. Knowing the hard times will pass makes them easier to endure, time does heal all wounds. Life does go on in all its glory and pain, all of its beauty and sadness.

When we deal with life's pain, whether it be the pain of death or any of the other myriad of life's pains, by coping to the best of our abilities and recognizing that it will pass, we must remind ourselves that not only do the painful times pass, but so do the most wonderful. When we live with a constant sense of the passing of each moment and the temporary nature of every situation, we can see the beauty of each moment that is not filled with pain, and there are so many more of those. We can come to realize that it is not life's big moments that are the most joyous, it is the daily miracles of life and living and loving that fill our hearts and minds. It is the simple things that bring the gentlest joy, the calm reverie we seek all too often "out there" somewhere.

Coping with pain, reflecting on life's temporary nature, and living in your moments can allow you to see beauty you may have missed for too many of your days. We can find ourselves deeply immersed in the sense of beauty that a magnificent sky can bring, we can cherish the warmth of clothes coming out of the dryer, every little moment can become significant, because truly your life is nothing more than the sum of every little moment. When you bring meaning and significance to all of your moments it becomes so much easier to see how beautiful most of them are, how joyous life really is, how passionate you can be with your life.

When we have learned to deal with life's disappointments by placing them in their proper perspective in the scheme of life and death, we find that we can choose more often to be at peace, we can choose happiness. These senses come from within us, and are ours to express. Once we realize the power is ours to harness, because we have challenged ourselves to deal with life's travails effectively, there is no limit. There is pain in life, but there is so much pleasure. There is so much beauty all around you. The very temporary nature of life makes all of our moments special and unique, look for them, look inside—it is where all answers are.

CHAPTER 3

Death Study

Dealing effectively with the pain inherent in life will ultimately mean facing mortality and life's transitory nature. This type of confrontation does not, however, have to come from a battle with illness or even from loss and death. Reflection and inquiry can help open a window to this feared arena and bring you closer to the passionate life that is yours to be experienced.

Throughout all of my adult life, I have been drawn to study death and have been blessed with the opportunity to do so in a defined and well thought out manner. While I had experiences with death as a child, my first inclination to explore the nature of death and its significance came in my teen years.

My parents were extremely involved in local community theatre and film work during my teen years. They had met in college as drama majors and had put that life aside to raise a family. Now they had found avenues to express their creative spirits and I was delighted to see this new side of my parents. They were really good. We daughters worked backstage, everything from props to wardrobe. Inevitably, I was compelled to try out for a play or two.

The first role I won was as the ingénue, playing opposite my father as his love interest. It was a silly bedroom comedy where the mother dates a younger man and daughter dates an older man. Fortunately, my father and I had no love scenes, it was all clean and funny. Though it was a strange pairing on a personal level, the aspect that mattered most to me was being with my parents as they did what they loved.

The second role I landed was as Emily Webb in Thornton Wilder's *Our Town.* Happily, my father played my father in this one. What was most stimulating to me about this play was not that I had the lead, but that she was dead throughout the third act as she laments people's inability to see what really matters. I won't say I was any good, I doubt I was, but I did pay attention to the lines and said them to the best of my limited abilities. My parents were wonderful given their skill level. They never belittled anything I did. They let me experience this my own way and allowed any criticism to come from other directions.

One of the greatest joys of this time in my life was the time it gave me with my parents, particularly my Dad. At a time when most kids pull away from parents, I was spending every evening with him. We were together every night, straight from dinner to a few hours at the theatre until we came home close to midnight. We would talk to and from the theatre about everything, often about life in general and certainly about matters such as death, given the role I had.

Right around the time the play wrapped, a friend of mine committed suicide. He was nineteen years old. I learned a few weeks later of the drug death of another friend. The 70's were rough on a lot of people. I did not leave my teen years thinking it did not happen to us, I knew better. As I aged and matured, death experiences continued to shape me and push me toward a more sincere appreciation for life.

Through the death, loss, and illness experiences that are inherent in life I grew into a person who embraced life more fully. I found myself evaluating choices and considering my path in different ways. Though I had a very fulfilling marriage and family life, the main ingredient that I did not have and that was valuable to me was a college degree. I entered school full time at the age of thirty-five. By this time in my life my kids were in junior high and high school and I figured they could spare me occasionally. It was daunting to consider entering the academic arena after such a long absence, but I felt if kids could do it, so could I. I can't recall a time I felt as nervous as I did when taking the required entrance exams at our local community college. The first step was the hardest, but once I jumped that hurdle, it all fell into place. I tried to focus on one semester at a time, as four years seemed so long a time to reach my goal.

I recall lamenting to my mother, "I'll be forty before I get my degree."

She characteristically replied, "Honey, you'll be forty anyway, do you want to be forty with a degree or without one?"

That made it easier.

I went to school with a vengeance. I did great, graduating summa cum laude. I loved it from start to finish. As I progressed through my undergraduate work and it came time to look at a major, I still did not know what I wanted to be when I grew up (still don't). I was being offered a scholarship at Chapman University and was looking through their catalogue at the possibilities. One major really piqued my interest, it was the Social Science of Health and Medicine. I looked through the titles of courses I would be asked to take and I was intrigued. Titles like: *Political Economy of Health and Medicine; Women, Health, and Healing; the History of Medicine; Gerontology; Community Mental Health*—these sounded fascinating to me. Though I was not interested in nursing, some sort of study in the field of medicine held a particular draw for me having worked in medical offices for ten years before my hiatus from paid work to raise kids. But one course title above all others sold me completely on this major: *The Sociology of Death.*

My course of study fit me perfectly. Chapman was great. The courses were interesting and challenging, but as I was preparing for my final semester I had still not seen *The Sociology of Death* in the course catalogue. I went to my advisor and let her know I was quite concerned as this was the one class I wanted most of all. She told me which professor taught it and suggested I check with him about it. I happened to see this professor on the quad one day so went over to ask him about it.

He said, “Yeah, I’m teaching it in the spring.”

I gushed, “Oh, good, because I am really into death.”

He said, “Yeah, my mother just died this summer.”

I was mortified, talk about putting your foot in your mouth. I quickly apologized, attempting to explain my comment. Fortunately, no apology was necessary he knew what I had meant.

The class was amazing, my favorite of all time. We studied how Western society views death, and responds to death. We looked at many Eastern texts and writers, we viewed films, had guest speakers, examining everything from near death experiences to coroner’s pictures, from grief recovery to slaughterhouse footage. It was a fascinating sixteen weeks, and it is the class more than any other that has had lasting and sincere applications to my daily life.

One of the more experiential lessons we were asked to participate in was to go to a funeral home and price everything, in essence plan our own funeral. Who knew you can do this any time you want? I was so intrigued. The people at the funeral homes are fine with this type of inquiry. It was great to see first hand how to do this business around death before you were in the middle of grief and pain. While in the class, I wrote wills for my husband and myself. This is something we keep current and in the possession of both of our kids. Being in that kind of class gave me license to speak freely about death at a time that it was not present in my life and that type of discussion and reflection became a norm for me. Studying death academically demystified it and truly helped when I had to face death in real life when it was most painful.

Beyond *The Sociology of Death* class, my field of study often examined death and loss, illness, and aging. While in school I had the opportunity to work with a hospice program, again learning immeasurably about a program that I have had to deal with more than once since that time. After leaving school, my work with a Crisis Response program led me to arenas where death and loss are a part of daily conversations, interventions, and actions. I have worked firsthand with people in the throws of loss and unspeakable tragedy. While the work is emotionally taxing, having the awareness I do of the reality of loss and death and the strength to discuss it openly, I feel I have brought some light to some very dark places. I have spoken to college students about my area of study, and death study in particular, and I have spoken to death study classes about what ongoing application and relevance this area of focus has had to my life. I currently work with high school students and whenever the talk turns to college plans I invariably tell them to take a study of death class if they ever can, as it will be the most important class they ever take.

Death study and preparation does not have to take on the structure of a formal course of study as it has for me. There are many ways you can visit this subject before you are faced with a death of someone dear to you. However, visiting this subject when you know you are facing a death near and dear to you can be imperative. It is never too soon to begin to prepare and it is never too late. I recently had the good fortune to meet a wonderful woman named Joanne. My sister, Allie, arranged that I should meet Joanne on a recent trip to Phoenix knowing that the book I was working on and this woman's recent experience would go hand in hand.

Joanne and her husband Kent had been married for 45 years, working together in real estate. Their marriage like all had it ups and downs, but she and Kent remained in love and close friends through everything. On September 23, 2003, three days after their anniversary, following a series of health travails and tests, Joanne and Kent learned that Kent had stage 4, primary liver cancer. With no history of drinking or liver disease the diagnosis was quite a shock not only to Kent and Joanne, but to all of the specialists treating him. Having lost a friend to a similar cancer, Joanne and Kent knew the road ahead was rough but they would be facing it together, wrapped in the love that had cushioned them through life's other challenges.

Joanne said, "Our lives came full circle. You learn to appreciate each other more fully and live each day fully grateful for the times you were given and blessed with the gift of time, although limited. We came to realize the gift each day brought."

They and their kids discussed things head on, they spoke candidly about what was going to happen and how they would face it. Their kids live all over the country, as so many families do these days, but they came together in the weeks following Kent's diagnosis and discussed everything, crying and loving as families can, paragons of support and love.

Joanne made an interesting decision in the midst of all this. She decided to enroll in a Grief Recovery workshop, something she had been in once before when facing loss. She felt she needed to gird up her strength to face what was coming. Joanne and Kent both knew Kent would not survive this cancer. They had discussed it often and openly. Kent fully supported Joanne's choice to study, reflect, and prepare. She began her multi week course, beginning to work through some of the grief issues she was already undergoing.

In late February Kent completed a series of treatments and blood work. He knew the process would cause him to fatigue considerably and decided to take a short trip to see his sister in nearby Mesa before the down side of the treatment hit him. An avid motorcyclist, Kent got his bike out and geared up to take the small, but very pleasurable trip to Mesa. Joanne had the expected concerns about him, but was so pleased he was feeling well enough to do something normal once again. She knew these times would be fewer and farther between, so she reluctantly supported his decision to have a bit of fun.

Joanne completed her final Grief Recovery class on Tuesday evening, March 2 as Kent prepared for his visit the next day. On Wednesday, March 3, while on his way to see his sister in Mesa, Kent was in an accident and killed instantly.

Kent's death, while expected due to cancer, came instead as a terrible shock. However, even in her pain and grief, Joanne knew he had been spared the final months of agony and anguish that would have resulted from his cancer. Joanne's numerous friends and family drew around her in a circle of support that sustains her still. She spoke very comfortably with me about this loss, this love of hers, and she felt her ability to do so was due in no small part to her attempts to prepare and face head on what was coming. Joanne's decision to reach out to study and reflect before death happened was one of the wisest things she had ever done and is something she would strongly advocate to any of us.

Death study and reflection, death preparation if you will, need not be something undertaken at the point of loss, or the point at which you learn of an impending loss—anytime it will help—anytime it is relevant. There are many routes you can take to review and reflect on this subject. You can enroll in local community college classes without pursuing a degree, some professors would even allow you to audit the class. For many of you college years are past, or college classes are not something you see yourself doing right now, no problem, you can study on your own.

In undertaking this type of inquiry you don't have to dwell endlessly on the personal losses you have had or that you will face if you are not comfortable with that, though they will inevitably come up as you explore this subject. To distance yourself from the more personal aspect of death and loss, why not start to question how we as a society face death? Think about how society influences how we view death and loss, think about how other cultures might do this in ways that could be beneficial to your life. I am not saying change your belief system or faith, I am saying don't be afraid to look at how others do it, you might be surprised at not only our differences, but how much we are alike. I have some suggested readings at the end of this text that might be a good starting point.

Further, aside from looking at the big picture of death rather than the smaller more personal and sometimes painful view, we can demystify the matters surrounding death. Make an appointment with a funeral home and go talk to them about options. They are perfectly willing to do this for you and it is far easier to go to these places under the guise of study than to visit through a mantle of grief and confusion. Very few of us will escape the necessity of dealing with one of these places at least once, why not prepare for it now? If a funeral home is too uncomfortable for you at first, just visit a cemetery. Take some time to sit and reflect on where you are and what such a place represents to you.

As I mentioned earlier, I had the good fortune to work with a hospice volunteer training program as part of my studies. This work brought me in daily contact with people who work with dying as well as with people who were dying and who had accepted that fate. All hospice programs utilize volunteers, it is one of the mandates from Medicare and insurance providers, at least it was when I worked with them. Usually the volunteers make regular home visits, reading to the individuals, writing letters for them or providing a small respite to their families. It is transformative work. Consider this option, but be sure you can commit what is asked. You will be well trained and given untold support. Not all of us believe we have the strength to hold someone's hand as they die as most nurses do quite often. Most of us are so far removed from death and dying that the very idea is foreign to us. We all know that just as babies used to be born at home, people used to die at home. Now 80% of all people die in a hospital. Somehow we need to reconnect to this experience, it is going to happen to everyone we know one way or another. Nurses are my own personal heroes, but it important to realize that we are not all comfortable in the medical arena. If working within a hospice program is not for you, accept that, but know it is an option. At the very least, learn about hospice programs. You can be almost certain you may be asked to consider such a program at one point in your life for someone you love or even for yourself.

Through reading, inquiry, and experience you can see for yourself how you can build strength to face the losses you will inevitably face. Consider expanding your horizons as far as death study goes. Review some of the recommended reading I have listed at the end of this book. If you don't want to immerse yourself completely in death study and reflection just consider adding to your annual reading at least one book that deals with loss, death, or society's response to death and it will help to allow the consideration of death into your daily life where it belongs. What ever you do, don't bury your head in fear of death it won't prevent it from happening. You have already made one step. You are reading this book. After all, it promises death in the title. See it's not so scary after all.

CHAPTER 4

Being Prepared, It Still Hurts

Reflecting on death, whether through study or experiences, as well as dealing with life's other pains effectively and constructively can help us in many areas of our lives, but none more profoundly than when dealing with death itself. Being prepared for the loss that is always inevitable should be a focus of our reflection. Sometimes however, we are very blessed and we are given clear signals that loss is coming. This period of grace before loss can allow some of the most profound interactions with loved ones that we will ever know. But don't misunderstand, being prepared does not relieve you of your pain.

We know that not all losses are alike, each relationship is unique, each person is unique. Very few relationships will hold the impact of the ones that we have with our parents. Therefore, very few losses will be like the loss of our parents. Though it is the more natural order that our parents die before us, it almost always comes too soon, there is so much more we want to share with them. Even when we are fortunate to have our parents well into our adulthood, it is never enough. It is not enough that they have known their grandchildren, we want them to know ours.

My father was diagnosed with metastatic prostate cancer in the summer of 2000, shortly before turning 67. I have vividly etched in my memory his voice on the phone when I asked if the test results had come in, he said, “Yeah, I have cancer.” He was very nonchalant about it, very matter of fact, very Dad. My heart froze for a beat.

We had seen Dad in May as he had traveled through El Paso on his way to my nephew’s graduation. His hip had been bothering him, something he had never really had trouble with. Dad had PSA tests every year, if not more frequently, and he had had some spikes in the level. I followed all of this very closely with my sister Allie, who is a nurse. The pain in his hip had already brought us serious concern and now the scan revealed that the cancer was in his hip and spine. Dad was very calm, very focused on his research into the options and very much in charge of his situation, in all again—very Dad.

Dad kept us informed of everything he learned at the doctor’s offices, he sent us articles he had researched on the internet, he described each and every pain and nuance of the illness, but what he did not talk about were the statistics, something Allie and I poured over. When cancer of the prostate is discovered while in the prostate the five year survival rate is about 98%, if it is discovered outside the prostate but in the same vicinity the five year survival rate is about 75%, but when it is discovered in the bone, one of the choice sites for this type of cancers to spread to, the five year survival rate is only 20%.

Now Allie and I are harsh realists, we knew this cancer would kill him. We cried together as we outlined how we suspected it would go. We figured a year or more of doing okay with it, then things would start to fall apart. He would get very sick and he would die. Ours hearts were breaking.

Allie is not just my sister, she is one of my closest friends. With only fifteen months separating us, we do not know a time without the other. We married within a few years of one another, have kids very close in age, worked for physicians next door to one another, our lives have followed a very similar path. In spite of that, we have lived in different states for more than eighteen years, though never allowing distance to create "distance." Allie and I began talking more and more frequently, constantly debriefing about Dad's condition. Our constant communication led us through one of the most important lessons we will ever learn.

Initially, Dad did great with his illness, living fully with our mom, the love of his life for nearly fifty years. They traveled extensively in their RV, often coming to see their kids who all resided in different states from their home state of Colorado. They were very active in their local and state RV clubs, having served in lead positions in the organizations. Dad had retired early at 57, and they had taken on this new phase of life with the same sense of adventure and spirit that they had approached everything with. They had moved us across the country a couple of times while we grew up, and had continued their professional moves after we had all married and left home. They had taught to embrace change and had kept completely connected to their daughters and their families despite distance.

When it came to Dad's illness, Mom and Dad both seemed to share it all with us, the ups and the downs, the pain and the times that felt okay. We talked constantly and they knew we were there for them. Allie and I were careful not to share our biggest worries with them. If they were to bring it up we would go there with no problem, but we tried to be sensitive about their feelings and at that point we were comfortable venting our angst to one another. Sure enough, just as Allie and I had privately predicted, Dad took at downturn at about 18 months into the diagnosis.

In May of 2002, he seemed to plummet in fatigue and pain, but he continued to get up and dressed everyday, they tried different medical options and things stabilized a bit. In July, however things got really bad really suddenly and Dad was hospitalized because the cancer had begun to spread up the spine and was causing inconquerable pain creating a potential risk for paralysis. He was to undergo immediate radiation to stop this sudden onslaught and the risks were great.

Allie and I started to feel frantic and far away as we talked nearly nonstop for a couple of days about what we could do. Dad had given his permission to his oncologist to talk to us, and we sisters had decided Allie should be the one who spoke with him. Her training as a nurse would allow her to speak more comfortably with him, in his own language so to speak. Allie learned of the serious risks of what the doctor called an "unfortunate complication" and we were filled with dread.

Mom and Dad never talked about the possibility of Dad dying, they seemed to stop just short of that when we discussed everything else about his condition. I had even tried to go see Dad the month before, but Mom had said it wasn't really a good time. This freaked me out a bit, we were always very close and felt at home with one another. Allie and I felt Mom wasn't facing the seriousness of the situation.

I had told Allie, "She can keep me away this time, but I won't be kept away if I feel I need to be there, we will just have to show up,"

Allie and I were sure Mom was going to be hit hard by reality very soon.

By now I was living in southern California and Allie and her family lived in Phoenix.

I finally said, "Look, I can just drive over to get you in Phoenix and we can drive up to Colorado Springs the next day, let's just go see for ourselves what is going on."

After bouncing phone calls back and forth all day, at about four in the evening, she said, "Let's do it, let's go."

I had packed and gotten ready, and off I went, arriving at her door five hours later. We spent an anxious night and headed out first thing in the morning and though we called them all along the way we did not let on that we were coming. We didn't want any drama with Mom saying it wasn't a good time, we needed to see our Daddy. We had called our other sister, Mindy, and offered to pick her up in Los Alamos, New Mexico where she lives. She was not comfortable seeing her Dad like this, and though Allie and I knew she would eventually have to, we did not push her, she would come around in time.

Despite an insanely ferocious hailstorm in northern New Mexico that permanently pock-marked my little SUV, we arrived at the hospital in Colorado Springs in twelve hours. We had finally confessed to Mom that we were coming when we were about 2 hours away, knowing she wouldn't turn us back at that point. We raced into the hospital room to see our Dad laying there, gray and frail looking.

He perked up a lot at seeing us, saying "You didn't need to come."

We said, "Yeah Dad, we did, sometimes it is not what you need, but what we need."

He was in the hospital for only a few days and things turned the corner a bit. Allie was able to organize his vast amount of medications and help address the serious constipation that accompanies the use of large amounts of pain medication. He was delighted to visit with us and we talked a lot about every aspect of his condition, every aspect that is except death. The only thing he said was that he figured he would mess around with this for fifteen years or so. I cautiously asked him if that was what the doctor had said.

He said, "No, I've never asked, I don't see the point in that." End of discussion.

Both my Mom and Dad knew my propensity for discussing death, they know my field of study, my embrace of the subject. I know they knew I was not afraid to discuss this, but it was a good lesson for me that not everyone feels the same way about it. Fortunately, I have very close friends, and Allie most of all, with whom I could debrief.

Allie and I returned to our respective homes feeling good about our visit and setting the precedent of our face-to-face involvement in his illness. Allie opened up even more dialogue with the doctor, speaking with him at the end of August when things weren't too good and asking if Dad was down to six months, the critical point at which hospice services can be utilized.

The doctor replied, "If that."

Allie asked the doctor why he hadn't told our parents this, to which he replied, "They haven't asked." It was his policy to reveal to patients only what they wanted to know. In his field, he knew that everyone approached their final journey in their own way.

Allie and I talked every day at this point, we knew this train was coming and we were frantic about Mom's awareness of the situation. We had mentioned hospice carefully to our parents and one afternoon our Mom called Allie to ask why she kept mentioning it. Allie cautiously told Mom we were concerned that Mom get the support she needed. Mom told her that if Dad thought he was down to six months it would be the "nail in his coffin." Allie got the message. We would avoid this frank talk of finality with our parents. We kept our other sister, Mindy, informed about the conversations with the doctor and she made a trip up to see them for their birthdays in September. Mindy reported back to us that Dad did not look good, his skin was that gray color that cancer sufferers get toward the end.

Allie and I went back to see Dad in early October, even visited his doctor with him. Dad was still up and dressed every day, though in a lot of pain and now doing physical therapy at the pool. I went with them one day for that appointment, feeling like an anxious mother at the side of the pool watching their little one learning to swim. He got in and tried so hard to do the simple exercises asked of him, screwing up his face in determination, grimacing in pain as well. Seeing him in his swimsuit, I could see how thin he had gotten, how horribly gray his pallor was. I felt like crying, but waited until I was alone to do that. I just cherished every moment with him. Back at their home, Allie and I massaged his legs when they hurt and his back, which constantly hurt. We loved him. There was nothing else we could do.

As Allie and I made the long journey home we discussed, as we often did, what we could do and what we could not. It was time to plan ahead to a memorial. We agreed that we would be the ones to write Dad's eulogy to speak it to their friends and neighbors. We started to discuss songs that might be played and began to consider the best way to honor him as he made this passage, we prepared in the only way we knew how. I made my plans to return to see Dad at Thanksgiving when I would be in Taos with my husband and kids, Allie arranged to come right after Christmas.

Thanksgiving brought heavy snows that kept us from driving up, so come hell or high water, I was determined we would go at Christmas when we were again in Taos.

I choked up all through my usual Christmas preparations. I baked my annual Christmas goodies with extra love and attention. I sent them to Dad with a note letting him know that I wished they were magic cookies and could fix what hurt. I knew this would be the last Christmas with my Dad. It was a painful time.

Dad had called me in early December to ask what he should get Mom for their 49th anniversary coming up on the 19th. I knew, as he undoubtedly did too, that they would not make their 50th. They had everything they wanted after a lifetime of hard work, I knew there was not a thing my Mom could want or need. I suggested that a heartfelt letter might be really nice. They had years of love notes and messages to one another, and as an avid collector of those momentos of my great love I knew these would be the treasures we would one day cherish most. He agreed that he had been thinking of that anyway, he still wanted a present though. We were thrilled to do anything we could for him. Both of my sisters had already undertaken the responsibility of getting gifts for him to give Mom for Christmas. He was not able to drive or be out on his own due to the heavy use of pain medication. They involved him in all the choices and sent things wrapped and tags for his personal signature to be attached.

On December 23, my husband, kids, and I drove up to see my folks. Dad was up as always, dressed and looking so cute with suspenders to hold up the pants his frail little butt could no longer support. Dad was anxious for me to run to the store to get a few more little Christmas gifts for Mom, silly things like playing cards and knee-hi hose for her stocking. Dad asked me get out the gifts my sisters had sent for him to give and he carefully wrote out the tags himself. Our parents had always made Christmas very special. It wasn't the gifts so much as the rituals and preparations that made it so much fun and Dad was determined to play out Christmas just like they always did.

We had a great visit, with our son Elias sharing a video of his summer teaching job in China. Dad could barely stay awake due to all the pain medication as he watched Elias climbing the Great Wall, but he grinned a silly little medicated grin at finally seeing his grandson on this trip he had followed so closely. He had emailed Elias throughout the journey, printing out and filing each email from his eldest grandchild. The kids and I took turns rubbing Dad's pained back for nearly three hours. Our children, Elias and Hilary, were honored to share this time with their Grampa Chuck. They knew how much he loved them, as he loved all of his grandchildren. Now they could return some of that love at a time when it was needed most.

When my husband had taken my Mom to the store, Dad watched me getting the dinner ready. He told me he wondered what the cancer was doing as it had not really been treated for some time, stating that he was just having his pain treated.

I thought, "Oh, he's ready to talk about what is happening." I braced myself and I gently said, "Do you wonder Dad?" leaving it open for him to say what was really on his mind.

He just nodded and quietly said, "Yeah."

We were not going there.

Dad said he thought that Mom did not really understand how painful it was. I had watched her, she was responsible for monitoring the medication as in his drugged state he could easily overdose. She responded very quickly to anything he said. She was like a soldier, she had the arsenal of weapons. She knew what to go to, what to try. She never belittled anything he said or dismissed any of his pain. I am sure she did know how painful it was, but she also knew there was little she could do about it. I just let him talk, did not try to talk him out of it. That seemed to be enough.

Dad was no longer able to climb the stairs easily to get to their room to sleep and they had decided he could sleep in the den on the hide-a-bed or his recliner as his comfort dictated. They had been doing this for some time and yet my Mom would completely strip the hide-a-bed each morning as if he would not be returning to it that night. Dad cried out for Mom in the middle of the night, another thing that had been routine for some time. She was up immediately with his pain medication, but I had heard him and was up as well, she sent me back to bed. Dad worried that his calling out had woken me.

Mom just assured him saying, "Honey, she's a mother."

In our world, as in most, Moms can hear whispers, sleep with one eye open, they can hear in their sleep, and it is they who take care of the sick and gladly accept the task of nurturing the entire family.

We had made plans to leave Christmas Eve afternoon, we had twenty plus people on the other side of the family joining us for Christmas dinner—life was going on. We spent the morning just visiting, and packed up to go. Dad was in pain, but that was as always. We hugged. I cried.

We all said "I love you."

I hugged Mom hardest and told her "Thank you for taking care of my Daddy, you just call and we will be here."

In response she whispered, "I know."

That was the closest we had come to the truth of the situation.

I cried much of the way home. Daddy was dying. We got to Taos and went through our little Christmas Eve rituals. My Daddy had always read us *T'was the Night Before Christmas* while I was growing up and then as an adult whenever they spent Christmas with us, which was about every other year. If he was not there, we read it, the very same book we had read since I was about six years old. We got out the book and as my husband started to read I started to sob. My daughter sat by me, holding me, crying silently. We laid out all our presents together, filled the stockings, listened to a Christmas CD. I know that in my sisters' homes similar scenes played out. We all tried to act normal, but it wasn't normal. Our dad was dying and Christmas was changing for us forever. It was a terrible Christmas Eve.

As we went to bed, the phone rang and Mom informed me that Dad had been admitted to the hospital. I wanted to come immediately. She said, no he was fine, just a small touch of pneumonia, they were going to treat him overnight and send him home in the morning. She was glad he was being well cared for, she would get some much needed rest herself. She promised to call if it was necessary. She knew we could get there quickly.

At five in the morning the phone rang again, it was Mom and Dad was not doing well. I told her we were on the way. I ran to wake the kids, asking stupidly what we should do about all the presents. You can get really focused on stuff that does not matter in a crisis situation.

Everyone said, "Throw the presents in a closet, let's go."

I called my mother-in-law, explaining the situation, but telling her we wanted them to have the Christmas dinner there at our house where it was planned. It was potluck anyway, my part was in the refrigerator and ours was the big house where everyone fit. My future brother-in-law, whom we had yet to meet, was due to arrive and was to be staying with us. I told them to be sure he still did, but not to leave him to rattle around there alone, my sister-in-law should stay as well. They agreed and off we went.

I cried and prayed to whole way, "Please let me see him before he dies, please let me be with him when he dies."

It was my most fervent wish since learning of his illness, if only I could be there when it happened, I could love him through. We arrived in just three hours, racing into the hospital room to find him sitting up, but uncomfortable.

Mom just said, "I think you better call your sisters," both live in other states.

I gave Dad a kiss and stepped out of the room with the cell phone. Mom had been keeping them posted, and had told them to wait until I was there to assess as well, however by the time I got there she knew it was time for them to come.

I told Allie, "Get here as fast as you can, call Mindy and tell her to do the same."

Dad was in pain, he spoke to us briefly, but started to be more and more unable to communicate as the medication got stronger and stronger in order to keep the pain at bay. I did not leave the room.

Allie was there by 2:00PM, racing into the room with her suitcase, saying "I hope you like this outfit, I think it is the only thing I brought."

Mindy and her husband were there by 5:30PM and one of the last things our Dad said was to her husband.

He said, "Fred, I'm a mess."

We all stayed around him, Mom would stroke his bearded cheeks telling him "I love you" and "I love this fuzzy face." She was fearless.

Once when one of the many attendants who came into the room said to her "I bet you don't want to be here on Christmas."

She lifted her chin, saying, "Where else would I be?"

She had known all along what was coming and we were only just beginning to realize the depth of her devotion to him as she helped us to understand she had allowed him to go through it his way.

Mom let us know that that morning when the doctor had called he had said that Dad's lungs were failing, that the only other thing they could do was to put him on a respirator asking if she wanted that. Mom told us that she had asked him if Dad was able to answer that question. The doctor said that he was and that Dad did not want one.

Mom said, "Then it is his decision."

Mom and Dad had agreed to this. Dad would decide for himself what he wanted and he did not want to be kept alive artificially. The doctor then recommended some books on loss and grief to my mom, at five in the morning on the day Dad turned the corner toward death. It was a nice thought, but the wrong time. The time to read those books, and they can be very helpful, is years before you need them.

It turns out that Mom had known how serious this was since Dad had first been diagnosed. She let us know that she had told him as she reached out to him how very sorry she was this was happening.

He had said, "Why? I'm going to live at least fifteen years with this."

She thought, "Okay, that's how you want to do this," and for two years she had cried only in the shower.

Mom would not shake his resolve or hers to discuss this even with us. If he was going to fight, she would fight with him. You will recall I told you my parents were actors. Mom told us this was the finest acting job of her career. We were stunned. She was as tough as they come and her love and respect for him was beyond measure.

As the day grew longer, Dad was crying out less and less, his final words were in replying to Mom's ongoing "I love you's."

He had gasped out "I love you."

As the night wore on, Mom started to fret about who might sleep where. We had grown into quite a crowd. They had a very big home. But, as I said, crises cause us to worry over insignificant things like where people can sleep and what to do about Christmas gifts. Allie told Mom that she did not plan to go home that night but would be staying at the hospital.

Given that she is a nurse, I knew what this meant, and quickly said "I'm staying too."

Mindy made it a fast threesome and that was that. We sent Mom home with the husbands and my children to get some much needed rest, she had done this for months on end, now it was our turn.

My sisters and I spent the most meaningful night of our lives at our father's side. Every cry was met with words of love, with gentle touch, with kisses and caresses. We kept assuring him we would take care of our mother, that it was okay to let go. Dad was agitated and fighting, but he would not win this time. I'm still not sure if he was afraid, I tend to think he simply did not want to die. He loved his life. He did not want to go anywhere.

Daddy had always wanted daughters, we knew this and each of us had a special closeness to our father who had wanted us and loved us. He wanted girls, but what he raised were women, strong, fearless women, who like their mother could love him through.

As the clock ticked past midnight Allie looked up and said, "Well, he didn't die on Christmas."

Our Dad gave us the most important Christmas we will ever have. None of us are very materialistic, but now more than ever we know the true meaning of Christmas. As horrifying as this Christmas might sound to some, it was the most beautiful Christmas I have ever had. It was *all* about family and love. We were not going to be able to stop this, but we could send him with love and that is exactly what we did. We worked with nurses on the ongoing increase of morphine until finally about two in the morning he cried out no more, he breathed in and out, though in a more random fashion, and he seemed comfortable.

We sisters talked with one another all night when he did not require our attention, and one or two of us were always holding on to him. Allie and I told Mindy of our plans to write the eulogy and do it and asked if she wanted to be involved as well. Though we are all very close, Allie and I are closer and in constant contact. Mindy had always said she could not stand to see Dad like this, so we did not want to pressure her or push her into areas she was not comfortable in. In spite of this, she readily agreed to do it with us. Her strength rose to the occasion as we knew it would. We are all of the same stock and we were seeing firsthand just how strong that was.

Our Mom, husbands and my kids returned by 6AM. We sisters had not slept one wink, and though we were tired, this had not been hard at all. We arranged to go home for a nap so the second watch could take over. There is no way to know how long these things will last, could be days, could be weeks. Allie, the nurse, was already planning how we could make the transition to home with hospice, we would be there as long as was needed. Hospice had been ordered and they were going to come see us in the afternoon, we went home to sleep.

Mom called about noon to say that Dad's breathing had changed and we should come back to the hospital. We hurriedly got up and dashed back to the hospital. We could see we would not need to worry about the transition to home with hospice. I went down to the nurse's station and asked that they stop the hospice folks from coming in to see us as Dad was going to take care of it on his own. We just wanted to be left alone with him. The staff was great, interrupting us as little as possible, coming and going quietly.

The day passed rather quickly and Dad was calm and unconscious. We all stayed around him throughout the day, always touching him, stroking his hand, his arm, his face. We listened to his breathing grow slower and slower, often with very long pauses in between until finally at 5:50PM it stopped all together. Allie quietly nodded to us and we knew he was not going to breathe again. Nurse that she is, she went to get the nurses, knowing they would have to be the ones to finalize what we knew. They respectfully came in and, listening to his chest, confirmed that our Daddy had died. He was 69 years old.

We rushed to each other's arms, handing off one to the other as we cried. We held onto Dad and thanked him for a lifetime of love and devotion, we stayed for over an hour. Mom said she wanted his wedding ring.

Allie said, "Then we should take it now."

They walked to my father's side and Allie gently slid off the ring that was as much a part of Daddy's hand as the veins that traced the back of them. She placed it softly in our mother's palm.

Mother closed her fingers around it saying, "I haven't held this for forty-nine years, he never once took it off."

This started a fresh round of crying, but it was as it should have been. We were there together. Mom was supported by those she wanted with her—her girls. She had held up in unbelievable fashion throughout the entire illness, now it was time to accept help and she was ready.

When we got back to the house, Mom explained completely how it was going to go. Dad would be cremated, his ashes scattered in the rose garden of the funeral home she had already decided to use. Mom asked me to make the initial contact with the funeral home, we were in my arena now and she gladly handed that over to me. We told her we wanted to do the eulogy as they were not a part of a local church and we could not bear a stranger from the funeral home talking about our Daddy. She readily agreed. It turned out we all felt the same way about how to deal with this business of death. We had never needed to discuss it after all.

Before turning in for much needed sleep, my sisters came to me and said I really needed to take my kids back to Taos for their Christmas as I would be staying on with Mom for as long as she needed. My sisters had managed very strange Christmas mornings with their families in spite of the need to make sudden travel plans, they wanted me to have the chance to do Christmas as well. I agreed as the funeral itself would be four days away. Our kids no longer lived with us, but we still do come together often and especially for holidays. It would be easier for my family to return to their lives and responsibilities knowing we had shared some quiet time together in the midst of all this.

Mom wanted to have her Christmas morning the next day for the cats. Yes, I said the cats. She and Dad had Christmas stockings and the rituals they had always shared with us were extended to the pets as well. Mom felt the cats needed this little special time. Maybe they did, she certainly did. Mom insisted we take turns opening Dad's gifts. It was painful, but it was beautiful as well. How many people get to open little treasures from their loved ones right after they have died? Mom cried, but enjoyed each thoughtful gift and gesture. We all agreed we would be donating Dad's gifts to charity. This was a sad Christmas, but a beautiful one to be sure.

I wrote out the first version of the eulogy, making sure to say all I wanted to say, to write about points I wanted to make. I left the editing and adding to the sisters, knowing we would all decide together what to say and how to say it. We agreed on some music choices and Allie and Mindy undertook the task of scoring the music and enlarging a photo for the Celebration of Life we planned for Dad.

As Allie's husband, Jerry and their children, Garrett and Marin, began their drive up from Phoenix, my little family and I drove back to Taos. We had our Christmas, and received love and warmth from that side of our family. Mom had requested no out-of-town mourners for Dad's service, she did not want to worry about other people's needs and accommodations. So my in-laws who would have wanted to be there, for they loved my Dad, gracefully stepped aside respecting our family's decisions and privacy.

We headed back to Colorado Springs again on Sunday for services Monday, making that trip six times in a week. We just did what must be done.

My sisters and I refined the eulogy and, at Mindy's urging, rehearsed it repeatedly so we could be as composed as one could expect. She was so wise to have us do this. Not only did it better prepare us, but our rehearsals ended up with laughing fits as we recalled the many puppet shows and circuses we had created as little girls, charging the neighbors three cents apiece to come see. Upon completion of our eulogy rehearsals we gathered up all the stuffed animals we could find and trotted them downstairs to tell Mom we needed boxes for cages and a coffee can to collect the money in. We all laughed, it felt good. We asked Mom if she wanted to hear it or read it before we did it.

She said, "No, surprise me."

The next day in front of about seventy-five of their friends and neighbors we celebrated our father and our mother and the beautiful love that they shared. We each spoke, breaking each part with music carefully chosen to reflect him and our feelings about him. It was glorious. My parents' theatrical presence flowed through each of us, and the love and respect we had for them both was there for all to see. Their friends were amazed at the strength of Chuck's girls. We know we made him very proud. It could not have been more perfect. We had taken the saddest time of our lives and because we were prepared we could make it into the time of honor and love that it should be.

We could not stop what happened to our Dad and being prepared does not mean it did not hurt. Of course it hurt, it still hurts. I still cry often for missing my Dad, but I do not have regrets. I did all I could, I said all I could, I loved him through and I love him still. I do not shy away from the pain I feel, there is no need. Dad earned every tear I have shed and will shed. He was a loving and wonderful man, my constant teacher, my biggest fan. I stayed with Mom for six weeks tending to the business of death. We took care of everything we could. She cried a bit in front of me, but seemed to prefer to do that alone. I had to respect her desire for that. I cried a lot in private and though I could have used a Mom to hold me in my pain, I was strong enough to turn to others and know that I would be comforted by my friends whenever it was needed.

Some time into our visit Mom shared with me the letter Dad had written her for their anniversary one week before he died. In it, he extolled all the virtues of their life together that we had celebrated in his eulogy. Though we never had a discussion of his own death, it was clear, we knew our Dad and what he would have been most proud of in his life. It was his marriage and lasting love for our mother. It was the fact that each daughter had found similar loves and had been joyfully married for well over twenty years apiece. It was that we had each lovingly raised our beautiful children with the respect and integrity he had raised us. My dad lives on in us, in his grandchildren. He did not need to discuss dying. He knew he had left the mark he wanted to.

The loss of my father was huge, but foreseeable, and therefore one that I could prepare for. Again, this does not mean it did not and does not still hurt. Being prepared does not mean being without pain. Be real, it will hurt like hell. I just did not add to my pain by allowing moments to pass without telling him I loved him. I visited as often as time and distance allowed, I rubbed his pain away to the best of my abilities, and I loved him fully. I loved him right through his death and I love him still today. I miss him, of course, but I did not compound my loss with regrets.

Every moment I was with my Dad I was with him. I did my best not to grieve the loss of him before he was gone and therefore rob myself of actual time with him still in my life. Of course I cried at the thought of his suffering and somewhat at the projection of my own, but I did my best to be present in the moment. Being prepared allowed me to participate in his care, to fully experience his death, to eulogize and celebrate him. Being prepared not only just when he was diagnosed, but for many years before, allowed me to love him more fully, to cherish him completely and it is that which brings some comfort at the time of my greatest pain.

Being prepared does not just apply to those deaths you can see coming. When someone is diagnosed with a terminal illness we are often granted time in which to prepare for the loss, time to consider our emotions and expressions, our communication and our intention. However, we must remember that death is always a possibility, death is the promise given to each and every person we know. Knowing this to our very core can help us be prepared all the time, it can help us to consider and reflect appropriately on our expression and communication at all times. It need not make you morbid and fearful, simply aware. After all this happens every day, in fact more than 150,000 times a day, death is absolutely a given.

By reflecting on death and facing life's pain head on you will find that you needn't be hurt further by being caught unaware. You need not be hurt further by overlooking an opportunity to be kind, an opportunity to express your love to someone or by not allowing someone to express themselves to you. Those missed opportunities will add unbearable grief to your pain. That is the part you can change. That is the part of loss that is in your hands.

Consider your behavior and your communication through the looking glass of death, always wonder, "If this were the last time I spoke to this person, how I would want it to go?"

It is far easier to find a gentler way of being in the world with this looking glass in place. Being prepared simply means being realistic about death and its place at the forefront of our lives. Instead of fearing the one thing we can count on, why not use what we know to seek a better way of facing life's inevitable losses? Why not use death as the powerful reminder that it is? Time here is precious, our relationships are precious, life is precious, treat them so—always.

CHAPTER 5

Facing Mortality

Being prepared for death and living in a state of awareness about life's temporary nature may be a conscious effort on your part, but for many of us it will be fostered and enhanced by a personal experience with mortality. Being prepared for death and loss means being prepared for your own death as well. If you have made a practice of dealing with life's other challenges and difficulties effectively and constructively, facing your own serious, potentially fatal illness will be something you do head on as well.

When I was thirty-three I had an illness that took up a lot of my time. I was weak and tired and bleeding nearly continuously, a problem I had never experienced. Though I became very pale, my first instinct was not to go to a doctor, it was to go to the Lancome counter to adjust my makeup. How stupid. But you know how it can be, you are busy with the kids, the home, work, whatever. If we can just make our face look all right, it will be okay. It didn't even occur to me that something was really wrong.

Upon finally seeing my internist, a friend whose daughter was on a soccer team I coached, we learned that not only was I anemic, but my white cell count was way below normal. She said she was going to have to have me see a hematologist as well as a gynecologist for the bleeding, because the white cell thing wasn't usual in excessive menstrual bleeding. I immediately asked her what it could be, having worked in medical offices for over ten years, I was not shy about medical matters and was always curious about which tests mean what. She hung her head and said, "Oh, I knew you would ask that," then she said "leukemia or aplastic anemia."

We talked this over, of course I knew what these two diagnoses could mean—bad shit. I was really calm. All I could think of was that my kids needed to be alright with this, that I would see them through whatever this was. Aunt Aurora was on my mind, I had never forgotten the promise I had made to myself that I would face life and death head on. Now, this was it. Medical terminology that heralds the most dire consequences was being used about me. Though we were still in the finding out stage, these kinds of words change your life.

I remember my very distraught mother asking me over the phone, as we lived in different states, "Why you?"

I replied simply "Why not me?"

Why not indeed, I had everything I had ever wanted, a great marriage and two beautiful children. Life was grand. Why should I expect to live forever too? No matter the outcome, when you have had to sit through weeks of appointments at the Northwest Cancer Center where you notice people look at your youth with the saddest eyes, when you have had to have a bone marrow test and surgery, you come out the other side a different person.

Long story short, I am fine. I spent six months being medicalized, poked, prodded, ultrasounded, and operated on and now I am as fine as anyone ever is, but I am different. For one, I don't have a uterus (which I truly do not miss), and for another I have never again thought that it cannot happen to me. Aurora's example of death and illness had stayed within me and when I was first asked to face my own death, I did. It will come up again, that's a promise, and I plan to face it head on then too.

Once you accept fully into your being that you can die, that you will die, that you might be dying right now, you never go back. It is like losing your virginity. I cannot be a virgin again, and I cannot be immortal again. This is not a bad thing, these are just phases in life after all. In fact, losing my sense of "it can't happen to me" is the best thing that ever happened to me. I thought I had embraced life before, but it is nothing like after. The experience of facing my own mortality most certainly fostered my interest in death's lessons. The passage through this ordeal stirred deeply in me the belief that it is moments that count, that every choice matters, and that every day is sublime.

One of my most treasured and growth-enhancing friendships is with a woman named Marcie. Marcie is a dynamic, brilliant, energetic, fireball of a person, full of ideas and action. Her ability to transform dreams into reality is completely unsurpassed. Marcie can take a mere suggestion and within the shortest time imaginable, single handedly create amazing and innovative programs and initiatives that enhance the lives of others. It is her life's work. She is the most honored and recognized person I have ever met. In her mere thirty something years she has amassed accolades and recognitions from two governors, a myriad of national organizations, state and local civic groups, and a whole host of political action committees and activists. Never have I known someone with the fire and energy this woman possesses. Marcie also happens to be a wheelchair user.

At the age of six Marcie developed a condition known as spinal myelitis. A hastily performed surgery, at the hands of surgeons who did not know as much as they should have, left her paralyzed from the waist down. Just three short years later her father, consumed by anger and anxiety over her fate, succumbed to pancreatic cancer, leaving Marcie and mother near destitute. To say Marcie's young life was hard would be a gross understatement. Despite all of this, I have never heard one word of bitterness from Marcie, she is one of the most joyful, loving, and spirited people I know. Our friendship was immediate and enduring, one born of similarities and a passion for life.

Many are the times Marcie and I have discussed death. She has supported me through several very significant losses and I have been with her through some of hers. She herself is forever reminded of life's transient nature, but rather than living in fear of the next possibility, she charges ahead and is determined to do as much as possible in whatever time she is given. Marcie is convinced she will die younger than most. Who am I to argue? Only she and her husband know the rigors and challenges she faces living her life every day. I have traveled with her, stayed in her home, spent days on end with her, but I still can only guess at what her life is really like.

Marcie never complains, in fact quite the opposite, she makes light of nearly everything. Sure there are frustrations, but they pass, and she goes on. I recall a phone call late one evening when Marcie and I lived in the same city. She had tipped off of the wheelchair ramp in her garage while at home alone. Being in a very heavy, motorized chair, it is not something she can right and move on with. Fortunately, Marcie had her phone on her, she had called her husband at work an hour away and he was on his way as she stayed wedged sideways between her chair and her van, something like a turtle stuck on its back. When Marcie explained the situation, I insisted I would come right over. She just laughed and told me no, she just wanted to have someone to talk to while she waited for her man. This was just business as usual for her, these things happen, you could only get so upset over something so routine.

I learned to take my cues from her, if she needed help I would give it, but her condition is not something we call attention to at all, it is insignificant in the matter of who she is and why I love her. More than once I have found myself telling her that a parking space she was about to enter was a space designated for use by people with disabilities, just like I do with any other friend who accidentally steers into one.

Marcie just rolls her eyes at me and says, "Yes, I know, it's one of the perks."

Since Marcie's mid thirties she has had to undergo a series of operations on her spine. She and her husband have connected her to the renowned Craig Hospital in Denver. The staff there just love her. Marcie will go with her laptop, send faxes out to the nurses station to be sent to her various clients, and juggle the hospital line and her cell phone, as she does her best to conduct as much business as possible throughout her hospitalization. Her husband is an absolute doll of a man who loves to help with anything she needs. As her husband is a physicist, she is the ultimate science project. Top it off with the fact that she has the most lovable service dog in the world, a smiling golden retriever named Morgan, and you can just see how the nurses must draw straws to be able to work with her while she is in their hospital's care. She is a one-of-a-kind patient and a one-of-a-kind friend.

On one of her surgical trips not too long ago, Marcie called me at home one day. She needed to tell me that she had developed a pulmonary embolism and that she had only a fifty percent chance of surviving it. Marcie said she needed to stay very still in bed for the better part of a week, that she could die at anytime from it and she wanted me to know she loved me. Marcie was very calm and matter of fact, as was I. We had discussed life's transitory nature time and again and now we were being put to the test. I told Marcie simply that I loved her as well and that I would hold her close in my heart always. What else can you say? I could do nothing but wait and love her.

Some time ago, Marcie drew up her will. She has asked me to be the executor should anything happen to her husband. Of course I have agreed. She has told me where the relevant papers are, what I am supposed to arrange, that type of thing. We are both comfortable with this subject. There are no technicalities to go over, we have done that, but there is always time to say "I love you" once again. We end every conversation that way, as I do with everyone I love. Sometimes you need to be very clear about it though. Sometimes you get a warning. You are lucky and you get the chance to square things up. Marcie did survive that major scare, but we both know it can happen again, anytime. We choose not to dwell on that. We choose instead to celebrate life and the joy of our friendship. We both know each day is a gift.

Facing one's own mortality is one thing, but being asked to face the mortality of one you love deeply is another. This will happen to you time and again though, so get used to it. You certainly don't have to like it, and you won't, but you can be prepared. One of the ways in which I have been able to face these losses or potential losses is by living in the moment and only the moment as much as possible. While I feared greatly what might happen to Marcie, I took each moment one at a time. I knew her husband was with her, and that he was the only one she would want to be there. I did not panic or grieve too soon. I sent out positive thoughts. I spoke with her openly about what was happening and I told her I loved her. What else can you really do? While you will face many losses, there will be times you don't have to go into the abyss, you may just be asked to go to the edge of it for a peek. This taking matters one moment at time has proved very helpful on some of the most difficult days of my life.

My wonderful husband, Lee, with whom I have shared my life for over thirty years, the man who had never, literally NEVER, been sick, came home one Thursday in the early evening with an outrageous headache. He had been struck suddenly with this severe head pain while in Sacramento that day on business. Lee told me he had stepped out of a meeting, his legs had felt weak and would not fully support him, and as he sat down a woman had approached him to see if he was alright. Lee had told her he was not, that in itself is uncharacteristic of him. He told her that he had a severe headache and she went and got some aspirin for him. Lee, being one who faces all kinds of daunting tasks with calm and ease, decided he just needed to get home. He hailed a cab, got on a plane and made the excruciating trip, head pounding. Lee arrived at our local airport, where his car was waiting and drove himself home rather than back to his office where he was expected for still more of a workday.

I was surprised to see him walk in as we had confirmed that morning it would be another of his many late nights, working until beyond 10:00PM. Lee told me what had happened and asked me to call his doctor, one he only has for the sake of required annual physicals. I was alarmed to say the least, but made the call as he laid down in his business suit and I gave him Advil and an ice bag for his head. We waited for the doctor to call back, as her office staff had advised us she would—the call never came. I kept suggesting we go to the emergency room, but he felt better lying down and did not want to have to sit up to go to the ER. His legs were starting to ache so we speculated that he might have a virus. I reviewed some medical books I have, looking at heart attack and stroke information, we determined he was not having either, but the sudden, severe headache was not good. I literally spoon fed him some soup as he could not sit up, and he fell asleep, ice bag on his head.

The next day Lee said he felt better, but would stay home from work, though he had to drive into L.A., about an hour away, to teach that night. Lee notified the coordinator that he might not make it so they could have a back up if needed—he is nothing if not professional. Now I try to hold my Lee with open arms, try to respect his ability to care for his own needs. I am not his mother. But after 29 years of marriage we all tend to assume a certain sense of responsibility for our spouses' well being. Lee did not want mothering, so at his request I went to work, but reminded him to take care of himself first and foremost. He assured me he would do no more than he felt he could handle.

Lee made it through the next couple of days okay, but the headache never really left him. It just sort of waxed and waned. By Sunday, he was feeling pretty good and thought we should go to the movies to take his mind off the headache and aching in his legs. I had given him a full body massage that morning in an attempt to relieve his aching and discomfort. He had enjoyed it thoroughly, but ultimately did not feel all that great. Just before we were getting ready to leave, Lee said, disappointedly, that he did not feel very well. He went back to bed and slept much of the day, you know—virus behavior.

Monday morning he still had a terrible headache and we agreed the doctor's non-responsiveness was not acceptable. He had to follow up and try to reach her again. I reminded him that a friend of ours was an internist in Orange County and not too far away. I said that perhaps he would be more sensitive to how uncharacteristic this was for my Lee. After calling Lee from my job at noon, I learned that he had reached Ravi, our friend the doctor, and that he was going to meet him at his office at 2:00PM.

When I got to my car at the end of my workday at about 3:15PM, my cell phone noted that I had 11 missed calls, all from Lee. I immediately called him. He said he had been unable to drive, so he had asked a colleague take him to Ravi's office and could I come get him. Of course, I was on my way. Not five minutes later, however, Ravi called to say he was putting Lee in the hospital as he needed a very thorough evaluation and that was the fastest way to get it. I was to go home and get Lee bed-clothes and the like and then meet them there.

Sensing the seriousness of the situation, I made several calls on my way home. I needed my own team for support. First, I called one of my best friends, Kim, who happens to be the clinical coordinator of the ICU where Lee was being admitted. She immediately arranged to go to the hospital though she was not due to be working that night. After notifying our kids, I got to the hospital to find Lee in a hospital bed being evaluated for viral meningitis or a brain hemorrhage which were the top two suspects we had for the sudden onset severe headache. Lee informed me that he had suffered what he considered a second episode with a very sudden increase in his headache pain, which was why he did not drive himself. He said that his legs had failed to function properly when he had arrived at Ravi's office building. Though I was extremely concerned, he was in good hands and exactly where he should be in a case like this. I just stayed focused on what was happening right then, not what could be happening. Ravi was there and tests were well underway. Lee was as safe as he could be, for the moment.

Tests were going to take a couple of days, and Ravi told me I could stay there overnight, but that it was not necessary. He said he was very close by and that the hospital staff would call him first if anything happened. I stayed with Lee all evening, and our son Elias came by as soon as he was free from work, a bit shocked to see his dad in a hospital. Lee was a total medical virgin, never having been hospitalized or medicalized in any way. I asked Lee what would make him the most comfortable overnight as I would gladly sleep in a chair in his room. He insisted I sleep at home as he would rest better. It was a long night, but we were still in the finding out stage and I did not want to get ahead of myself. My mind kept venturing to the consideration that this was it—our time together was over. I struggled to stay in the present moment by constantly reminding myself to do so. It was *not* easy.

The next day I was at the hospital bright and early, Lee was sleeping and medicated with painkillers as well as a sleep aid. Anyone who has ever been in a hospital knows that it is no place to rest. I sat quietly and read, did some yoga, and waited. At about noon Lee awakened more fully and we learned from the neurologist that nothing really substantial had been found with the CAT scan or the MRI, so they were proceeding to a lumbar puncture, which he would do right there is Lee's room. I held Lee's hands as I watched the doctor draw the cerebrospinal fluid from his spine. I noticed it was bloody and thought it was supposed to be rather clear (having worked with doctors for ten years I have just enough knowledge to be aware but useless). The doctor very calmly drew fluid from four places on his spine. All were bloody.

He then stated, calmly, "Well, we know you have had a brain hemorrhage, so we are going to do an arteriogram next."

He left the room. I took a deep breath, could feel the shaking deep inside, fear was coming. I stepped out to call the kids, this was getting scarier and they had the right to be in the loop. I was getting nervous, but wanted Lee to feel as calm as he could. He did not need drama from me. I told our daughter, Hilary, that she needed to look at flight information as she lived two states away, and she would probably need to get to us.

Upon my return to the room, the nurse came in and said, "You know we are transferring him to the ICU immediately?"

We did not. Now this felt very scary. I contacted Kim again. She was following everything from home after being around the first evening and though she was due to work that night's shift, she came in immediately that afternoon to oversee his care on her unit. Kim is a wonderful, loving and intimately close friend. I could not have asked for better support at a time like this. The gods were smiling on us to have placed him in this hospital, nowhere near the closest to our home, but where friends like Ravi and Kim could be so professionally, as well as personally, valuable to us.

Upon arrival in the Intensive Care Unit, the pace changed considerably. There was constant nurse attention, constant monitoring, absolutely no privacy as the room had big glass windows right in front of the nurses' station. Preparations were underway for the arteriogram and one of the nurses said, "Oh, you'll need 'Advance Directives'," which they brought in to us and told us we would have five minutes to fill out. I quickly learned that these are papers giving over medical power of attorney for things like removal from life support, organ donation, removal of feeding apparatus, administration of pain medication even to the point of hastening death, etc. Heavy shit.

I reflected on my mom's bravery in the face of the loss of my dad. I knew full well this was what I could be facing. Just as my mom wanted my dad to make his own decisions if he could, I wanted to be sure Lee did the same. We were not just going to sign these blindly. Calling forth any strength I might have, trying to stay in the present moment, I read each clause to Lee. I was determined that we both fully grasp what was happening and the gravity of what was being signed. This was the darkest moment of my life. The abyss was looming and it was frightening. As painful as this was, I knew that if this was it I was going to soak up every second with my Lee man. He was not going to have to see me falling apart. I cried a bit as we filled this out, this was really serious stuff after all, but I did not go into the abyss it was not time yet.

Lee held my hand and said, "You know what I want. No vegetables. No life support. It has been a great life. Thank you. Bright flows the river. And if you find someone who is nice to you, move on."

This was the last thing I wanted to hear, but in retrospect I have realized what a kind thing this was for him to say. What a wonderful man he is.

We were hustled down to the room for the arteriogram. Kim, assigning herself as his nurse, was by his side the entire way. The procedure and its risks were explained to both of us. Its purpose and potential findings were pointed out. Then the doctor told us we could say goodbye and stepped aside. We both knew Lee might have to go straight into neurosurgery and that he might not return from that kind of surgery, or return from it the same. We preferred to say we would see each other later and we kissed a good long time. It just broke my heart to have to walk away, but the last thing he would see on my face was a smile, the words would be those of love. The tears were there, no sense in hiding them, but they were not tears of anguish and anger, just tears of sorrow and fear. They did not dominate the message or the messenger.

I sat waiting in a specified waiting area where another family struggled with their reality, all of them crying, sobbing and clinging to each other. When you are in your own pain, it is hard to find room for the pain of others. I remained in my own little corner, praying, meditating, and focusing on my love of my Lee. Kim came out when she was no longer needed and held my hand. She knows me well and knows how I face things head on, but I will admit to telling her I did not want this to be happening. However, it was.

Whatever the outcome, this was very serious. I was being asked to look into the abyss of life without Lee. I did not like it, not one bit. By staying with the present moment and not getting too far ahead of myself in the "what ifs" I could cherish what was and not fear too much what could be. Kim kept telling me she couldn't believe how well I was handling it because if it were her she would have been freaking out.

I teased her saying, "Cut it out, you're making me feel like I don't understand the gravity of the situation."

I am strong, but despite my attempts at levity this was testing any limits I have ever had. The doctor came out after about an hour. He said that Lee did have a subarachnoid hemorrhage, though not an aneurysm or other anomaly that caused it. He further explained that Lee would have to be evaluated by a neurosurgeon, as brain surgery was still a possibility, but the biggest fear, an aneurysm had been ruled out.

Elias and his friend, Lorin, who is like our second son, came by to see him, shaken at this new reality. That night the neurosurgeon still had not seen him as he was tied up in emergency surgery, so Lee sent me home about 10:00PM so he could get some rest. We were told that Lee would be in the ICU for at least five days even if he did not have brain surgery. That was one hard night for me, home was forty-five minutes away and I was completely alone there. I slept fitfully and woke up crying, dreaming he had died, experiencing all the anguish and fear I was repressing when awake while I slept. I got up at about 4:00AM and did a calming yoga tape, centered myself, and headed back to the hospital. Lee's neurosurgeon had come in before I got there, he had told Lee that he usually had two choices, one being brain surgery which you have a 50/50 chance of surviving and the other being a much less severe hemorrhage which is the kind you watch. This is what Lee had. We were relieved to say the least, but it was a long, slow recovery. It helped that my daughter, Hilary, came to be with us throughout it.

It is worth mentioning here that one of the hardest parts of all of this for me was a major difference of opinion Lee and I had over disclosure. He had insisted that I not call his parents and sisters, and no one from his work, where he is the big boss. Now his work was no problem, that is his business, but his mother! This was tough, but he was adamant about it. Lee said he could not deal with her being upset. He could not face her worry and concern. I tried everything I could to gently persuade him, but ultimately had to hold my respect and love for him first and foremost. I was not going to argue with someone with a brain hemorrhage and I would never make that call behind his back. Lee was in terrible pain and I would not add to that. Only after he found out he did not have to have brain surgery, and after he was sure the crisis part seemed to be past, did he call his mother. Lee had been in the hospital for four days, three in the ICU. He did tell her everything and now so could I. They are a beautiful, loving family and don't waste time on blame and anger. They were shocked and very concerned, of course, but other than humor and ribbing there were no repercussions. Lee's health was and is all that matters to any of them. He is loved and cherished by every one of them. I would have endured any repercussions that might have come however. The decision not to call them had been thought out and considered, it was no casual or easy choice, but ultimately my respect for Lee came first.

Lee and I did learn, after his weeklong hospital stay, that only 30% of people survive paracerebral hemorrhages such as his intact. We were very lucky—this time. Lee's condition was unpreventable, unforeseeable and is no more likely to happen again than that it happened in the first place. We learned that his arteries are clear as could be, his heart is like a 25 year old athlete's, and his cholesterol is down 128 points from 6 months ago due to changes in diet. In all, Lee is the picture of health we always thought he was. But this was a reminder. Life is tenuous at best. Tomorrow is promised to no one.

Being at the edge of the abyss afforded Lee and I a view of what lies ahead for one of us—life without the other. But we did not have to go there yet. I can tell you for certain, nothing has ever felt so good as climbing into bed next him once he had been transferred out of the ICU and just lying beside his warmth. Lee was still having a severe headache, but things were getting better and I could just lay beside him and feel him breathe. There has never been a sweeter moment. My tears just flowed silently as he slept, my joy and relief so great they could not be contained. My struggle to remain only at the moment I was truly at had worked. I had not had to go fully into the darkness that the loss of one so dear will mean to me. The view was frightening enough, but the anguish could be avoided by remaining calm and focused on what was not what could be. Many months have passed and I still get tears in my eyes when I reach over and hold his warm, broad hand. The life in him is so precious to me. His mere presence is a gift.

By facing mortality through our own personal illnesses as well as through losses and potential losses, we can find ourselves better able to face everything. Life's greatest challenges are not so great compared to death. This does not mean we won't get frustrated and anxious at times, of course we will, but we can try to let these emotions pass rather than cling to them as if they will hold us up. These emotions do not hold you up—they drag you down. Love is what holds you up. We must love as fully as we are capable of on any given day, some days we will be better at it than others.

By trying to stay in the moment you are asked to be at, you can catch yourself before going too far into the abyss. You can learn to face each decision as significant, because they are. Everything we do, every response we give, every word we speak—is a choice. We must understand that we are not in control, but we do make choices and those choices impact the quality of our lives and relationships. Bad things will happen to us, we can't change that, but we can choose how we will respond. Though we are not in control, at the very least, death should remind us of that, we can impact the quality of our lives. What we can do is live fully and with love, speak carefully and with intention, choose wisely and with forethought, the rest will happen as life does.

CHAPTER 6

Physical Death, Physical Life

Facing mortality through study, loss, death or illness can bring us closer to many of our truer feelings and inclinations as human beings in this physical plane. While many of us will feel called to explore our spirituality, one thing illness and death brings very close to our consciousness is the reality of our very physical and fragile nature. A brush with the truth of that fragility can bring us further in exploring the physical boundaries we exist within and in challenging those boundaries and assumptions of limitation.

A very good friend of mine, Carol, was diagnosed with thyroid cancer at the age of forty-three. She was living at the peak of possibilities, happy and in love with her husband of two decades, free of the restrictions of children to raise, working at stimulating and interesting work, traveling frequently and enjoying adventures, in short—loving life.

When Carol was told of the diagnosis, she and her husband were right in the midst of preparing for a white water rafting trip through the Grand Canyon. She had been training in the gym, knowing that rafting can be physically demanding. She was preparing herself for the feat in her usual enthusiastic fashion. As Carol's doctor explained the need for immediate surgery to be followed by radiation therapy, she explained that it would have to wait until they returned from their long planned adventure.

Her doctor wisely went ahead and scheduled things for her letting her know they could alter the plans, but that after she had reflected a bit on what he had told her she would probably want to get the treatment underway as soon as possible. By the time Carol and her husband reached the elevator, it hit her—she had cancer. White water rafting would have to wait.

Surgery revealed three tumors on her thyroid and the surrounding lymph nodes. All were removed and Carol was sent for radiation treatment using a massive dose of radioactive iodine that would be ingested. The radiation experience was unlike anything she had ever encountered medically. Carol was led to a strange sci-fi like room, all lined with plastic, strangely sterile with lead lining the doors and lead drapes between the door and the bed. Carol had to be isolated for 24-48 hours while her body assimilated the radioactive iodine that would target the site effected by the cancer. Nurses wearing lead vests gave her the substance to drink after which they scanned her and the surrounding area with a Geiger counter-like device, which clicked loudly indicating that radiation was present. Carol said she felt like a contaminated glow-worm. She had to be scanned periodically to follow the body's absorption of the material. When it was clear, Carol could leave. Anything she had brought with her had to stay behind due to radiation contamination. To say it was weird, and a bit intimidating, would be a tremendous understatement.

Following her release from the quarantine, Carol tried to resume a normal life. She felt pretty good, and though she was told she would be a bit tired she did not realize how different her body was until a couple of weeks later. Carol's husband took her to La Costa, a wonderful spa in southern California, for a bit of R and R following her ordeal. They both had much to be thankful for with the treatment behind her. It was time to have some sort of vacation, though perhaps not white water rafting. At the spa Carol noted a small track and decided to give herself a little quarter mile run to start to rejuvenate her body. Much to her surprise, she could not even make it around the track once. She was tremendously depressed by that reality, but determined to go a bit further each day on that same track. Carol came home determined to increase her stamina and push herself further toward feeling fit and healthy. She became a regular at the gym, working with trainers and following a healthy diet and exercise regime. However, each year when it came time to go for the scan to follow up the possibility of recurrence of the cancer, she found herself depressed and anxious, fearful at the potential of cancer's return.

On a flight to Tahiti with her husband, Carol considered the annual emotional slide she was experiencing around her cancer history and she made a pivotal choice. Carol decided she should train for something really big, really challenging in order to take her mental focus off of what could happen and onto what she could make happen.

She asked herself, "Am I going to be a participant in life, or am I going to watch?"

Carol decided to train for a marathon. Beginning in March of 2001, Carol began her training, running at least six days a week, three miles a day, six to seven miles a day on the weekends. Now Carol and I had been a lot alike. Women of our age and generation often dabbled at fitness. We were more active than our parents' generation, but had never truly been athletes. Mind you, at this point Carol was forty-seven years old. Well, in October of 2001 Carol ran her first marathon, 26.2 miles in 4 hours and

41 minutes. She can cite the time it took her like women can cite their labor times. Carol has run two full-length marathons and several "shorter" runs. I put this in quotes because to me ten or fifteen miles is not a short run, it probably isn't to most of us. Further, Carol has been cancer free for six years now, passing the all important five-years-clean mark. More importantly, Carol no longer falls into a depression at the annual scans and tests she faces. She pushed herself to physical limits few of us will dare. She found new boundaries and possibilities for her physical body and in so doing, new boundaries and possibilities for her spirit as well.

Now most of us will not run marathons, I for one most surely will not. But Carol's experience with new possibilities and pushed limitations in the face of mortality inspires me. It reminds me of the lesson death brings to us about the physical side of this thing we call life. Life as we know it is physical, death reminds us of that. At the very least the part of life and death that we grasp the most fully is physical. Why not use that reminder as a transformative tool?

While we are very clear that we experience pain, illness, and death physically, we must remind ourselves that we experience joy, health, and life through our physical senses as well. My husband likes to say we are spiritual beings having a physical existence. I like this. No matter what your sense of spirituality, there is no denying the physical side of our existence. However, life is not merely physical it is deeply and beautifully sensual. It is our visual sense that perceives the magnificent sunset or the changing autumn leaves. It is our olfactory sense that picks up on the smell of our love's most favored fragrance, that rushes to our memory the coziness of a real wood fire, that brings us to salivation as we sauté chopped onion and garlic, which seems to be the beginning to nearly everything I cook. It is our sense of taste that revels in the flavors of wonderful food, the tang of a lemon, the ecstasy of a mango. It is our sense of hearing that listens to morning birdsongs, the laughter of children, or the transformative beauty of music. It is our sense of touch that feels the softness of a baby, the coolness of diving into a pool of water, or the magnificence of running our hands through my husband's luxurious hair (though only I get to do this last one).

In order to live passionately with the promise of death we have to use that reality to open up uncharted territory, to bring out more fully the possibilities within the confines of this physical realm. If we want to explore and expand our relationship with the physical and sensual nature of our existence we have to step back and review our place within our culture and the limits that we place on ourselves when it comes to expressing and fully experiencing our nature. As a student of sociology I was often asked to examine the nature of being within society, the constraints and confines of socialization and civilization. Many of these inquiries led to the realization that particularly in western society we deny our very nature, we try to place ourselves above it. The western denial of death is perhaps the most harmful component in our long quest to rise above nature, to not truly be a part of it. And where has it gotten us? We still die, though now it is with guilt and fear.

In examining our western cultural heritage, I began to take note that the way we speak about death on a daily basis added to our separation from nature and death's place in the cycle of life. For example, we frequently will say that someone's life was saved, but never say that their death was really just postponed. We read that 50% of all Americans die of heart disease, but we are never reminded 100% of Americans die. We are not expected to be ever aware of the truth of our existence—that we die. We are not acculturated with this truth. We avoid it. We act as if it is a surprise when we learn of loss and illness. We always ask when we learn of a death, how old were they? We want to figure out how far we are from that age or to determine if this was a "fair age" for such a thing to occur. We ask about their personal habits. Did they smoke or drink? What was their family history? It is as if we want to see how we can beat this by avoiding the things they might have done or if we have a family with a slightly different health history. We are not accustomed to recognizing death events as normal everyday occurrences, as inevitable and foreseeable.

Without going into an entire inquiry into our western cultural heritage, though it is something we should all do—we can see through a few small examples the force of this repression of nature that is so much a part of us. Our western heritage is one with an extreme emphasis on reason and a de-emphasis on matters physical. We are expected to rein in and control our natural physical qualities with reason. The tendency to put the cerebral over the carnal is all pervasive in western writing and thinking. Every attempt is made to rationalize and explain completely all that humankind is, all that we experience, be it love and sexuality, or our connection to the rest of the animal kingdom or the planet as a whole, or our very place in nature—which in western philosophy is decidedly above it. It is as if by finding reason and rationality supreme, we can deny our animality and convince ourselves that we are different and apart from nature.

We don't just do this with death, or rather the denial of its centrality to our existence. We do this in all matters physical or carnal. It is women's very earthiness and connection to their nature—menstruating, birthing, lactating and the like that has helped to sustain our secondary status in a world where men struggle to dominate nature. This reminder of the physical side of us, the only side we can truly know fully, appears to strike such fear into the collective hearts of men whose struggle to be better than nature, above nature, that it takes them away from the essence of existence. What is most sad about this predilection of man (and I use the gendered pronoun purposefully here) to place themselves above nature is that in our fervent desire to be important, we have lost sight of the simplicity of living and dying and the importance of that simplicity.

Perhaps the most damaging aspect of the repression of our nature is that in turning away from the fact of our nature, the truth of our animality, we are then turning away from death as a tool for living fully. We are not merely setting ourselves up for a big crash when it comes to facing death and loss. In repressing our nature, we are not just turning away from death, we are turning away from life, physical life, which is ours to cherish and enjoy completely. To embrace death as the learning and growth opportunity that it is we must look at the physical aspect of our nature, after all it is the physical aspect that dies, we really don't know about the spiritual part. Many have faith about the spiritual aspect of death, but we don't truly know. We do know the physical part dies therefore, should we not allow the physical part to live as fully as possible? Since we are having a physical experience, a carnal existence, why not make the most of it?

We need to fully use our senses to truly live passionately. We are in these physical vessels, why not see what they can do? To turn your journey toward more passionate living try a few simple things that can help you see the repression of sensuality and physicality that is inherent in our culture. Use your senses as fully as possible. For example, try eating with your hands one entire meal, and not a meal that is always eaten with your hands like a burger and fries. I mean a salad, rice or pasta, fish or chicken and dessert too, preferably something really messy. Just skip the tools, see what it feels like. If you really want to see what it is like to go outside of your comfort zone, do this in public. If you are more nervous than you need be, just do it at home, it doesn't matter, just try it. Okay, what did it feel like? Is it not one of the most sensuous things you have ever done? You don't need to eat this way always, do what you are comfortable with. This is just giving you an opportunity to experience your senses in a new way, to view how we separate ourselves from our nature. This simple exercise can demonstrate how the very tools we use daily tend to repress the sensuous and physical dimensions of our lives.

Now here's a really challenging idea, try to live without the TV for one day, or better yet a week. I know, the TV uses your sight and your hearing, but you know as well as I it does not stimulate your mind or fully involve your senses. Try just listening to music all day, and while you are at it burn some scented candles or incense. It might seem hard or boring, but give it a go. Try reading a book or just enjoying your own thoughts. If you don't have any, books or thoughts, be concerned—you have a lot more work to do! If nothing else, it will help demonstrate to you how much you look outside yourself for stimulation. I mean come on, how passionate is watching TV? I don't mean never watch TV, I just mean question yourself about it, is it really fulfilling to you or is it a habit?

In the quest to embrace a fully sensual and physical life we have to consider how and what we eat. I have a particular reverence for food. I love it. I love to eat food. I love to prepare food. I love to share food with others. I always express my love and concern to others with food. Food is energy to me, it is life, and ingesting with respect is an act of worship, it recognizes the divine connectedness of all life. For many years before eating I have reflected on the food's origins, on the path it has taken to get to my table. I am always grateful for the blessings of nourishment we have here in America. I eat mindfully and with a grateful heart for the choices and options available to me. I loved studying biology and nutrition. It reminded me that everything we ingest is broken down to the cellular level by our bodies. This certainly caused me to consider everything I put in my mouth. I do not proselytize to others about eating. Again, life is a personal journey, but everyone notices sooner or later my special relationship to food. Inevitably, I am asked for advice or suggestions about what to eat for certain responses or reactions, certain ailments or conditions. I share what I know, cook for others all the time and revel in the joys of food and eating.

My point is this—in this physical existence you must eat, but what you eat is up to you. How you eat is up to you. Whether you overeat is up to you. In a country where fifty percent of us are obese, this element of our inquiry takes on new meaning. Examining this aspect of our nature and its impact on our lives, as well as the fulfillment of our potential, becomes paramount. Ask yourself what kind of energy you want. What sources do you want to be closest to? Eating should not be a mindless act undertaken when the stomach complains. It is at the heart of our connection to other elements of nature, something dies in order for you to live. Yes, even vegetarians have to know that we kill the lettuce to eat it. Life is a cycle of death and living, and everything is linked.

Now, we are feeding this physical body, but are we really using it? Again, with the recent revelations about the harsh reality that half of Americans are obese, not only must we pay attention to our source of nourishment, we know that we should move more. Do something physical for yourself—anything. Walk, bicycle, yoga, whatever, but get up and move. Try to see your body for the wondrous machine that it is. It is a gift, this physical creation, love it and appreciate it. Yes, you're still going to die one day, your physical body will stop functioning, but shouldn't you feel as good as you can in it while you are in it? There are multitudes of options for physical exertion and exercise. Consider one, consider several, but do something with this vessel you have been graced with, you are its keeper. While physical activity may lead us to a firmer, more toned body that should not be the goal. We should use our bodies physically because it is healthy and reverent of our physical essence. No matter what our spiritual leanings, we can respect the notion that our bodies are perfect as created, that they are what we are supposed to live in right now, that their functions are not merely accidents of nature. We can recognize that our bodies are manifestations of life, and showing honor and respect to that manifestation can transform your experience of living.

D.H. Lawrence wrote that "the body's life is the life of sensation and emotions... All emotions belong to the body and are only recognized by the mind." He was uniquely in contrast to the history of western thought which demands that we control our emotions, control our body's responses and desires with our mind, with our will, and with our reason. Many of us know D.H. Lawrence as the author of *Lady Chatterly's Lover* and many other works, renowned for his explicitly sexual writing, and of course he was. His writing is most unique, however, not so much for its depiction of explicit sexuality, but for the respect and reverence he placed on sexuality and sexual expression. This is the ultimate of our physical gifts, sexuality. This above all senses unites us to that which is divine, to the universal energy of life.

My mother was recently telling a friend that I was writing a book, which of course led to the inevitable inquiry as to what it was about.

Mom said, "Death—it was either that or sex because that is all she talks about."

Well Mom, only I could write a book about death and manage to talk about sex! The truth is I am able to speak openly about all matters physical—eating—exercise—sex—death. You see death and sex are not so far apart. They are simply a part of the physical aspect of our existence, but more than that they are part of the spiritual essence of humanity. Respecting and revering your physical existence demands that you place at the forefront death and its promise, but as I have told you already, life's passion and death's promise are flip sides of the same coin. To live passionately you will embrace many elements of your physical existence and you will inevitably embrace your sexuality as well.

When we respect our vessels and embrace their gifts, we are capable of living more fully and with passion. Look with fresh eyes at the beauty of everything around you. Appreciate color, light, and shadow. Notice things in your daily space you had not noticed before. Taste with care, pay attention to what you eat and drink and how it makes you feel. Embrace your sense of smell and the powerful memory marker smell holds for you. Fill your world with smells that appeal to you, and notice how potent this sense really is. Listen with appreciation, don't just have the television as background noise, use music to create the effects you are seeking. Touch with tenderness. Use touch to heal and comfort others, as this will ultimately bring healing and comfort to you. Hug often and with love. Recall always that everything is temporary. Appreciate what is now.

The death you will face one day will be physical—that we know for sure. Should you not also recognize that the life you face right now is physical as well? What amazing and wondrous vessels we occupy. Use them to their extreme. Treat them with reverence and care. Learn all you can about how they work, how you can best nourish and protect them. Learn what feels good and right for you. Dance, move, breathe in and out. Your body is a gift, one meant to be enjoyed and savored. Until death comes for you—live. Oh, what pleasures await you!

CHAPTER 7

Divinity and Spirituality

Embracing death as the learning tool that it is will not only lead us closer to the physical dimensions of our existence, it will inevitably bring us to consider matters of spirit and the essence of life. It is impossible to separate death and loss from questions about what happens next, what happens after. I would never attempt to address these questions, I don't know. What we can explore is the nature of spirituality, the essence of divinity as defined by we humans.

For me spiritual development and query began early in my life. As a teenager in the seventies, I fancied myself at the edge of the era of questioning authority. I was coming of age seeing young people challenge the status quo, change the voting age, question the draft, and denounce the notion of war. I saw the generation a few years older than I starting to explore other religions, other philosophies, to challenge traditional Western approaches to life. The Beatles were meditating with gurus and we were reading Kerouac and Vonnegut. We were "oh so cool." At the same time my coolness was forming, my parents had me going through the traditional Lutheran confirmation process. This involved more than two years of study with the church, at a parish where studying other religions as well as our own was part of the process. Questioning was allowed and encouraged.

I can remember vividly talking with my father and a great uncle who was visiting and saying that as I was studying religion I found myself questioning the existence of God. I told them I thought I was agnostic, one who did not believe or disbelieve, but one who just did not know. They talked this over with me intelligently, with genuine interest in my perspective and interpretations. Both told me this was fine. I loved this about my family, inquiry was always encouraged. Faith was part of our family, but we were allowed to develop our spirituality in our own way. I was fortunate to have an open and supportive family where the acceptance of others, respect for others, and attitude and actions mattered far more than organized, formal religious structure.

I have a very close friend who is a very active member of one of the largest Christian churches in the nation. She participates in bible study, youth groups, numerous committees and activities, and has traveled the world to spread good works and share her faith. I have family members, to whom I am very close, who are devout Catholics. They find solace in the sacraments and rituals of that faith. I have a son who has tattooed the symbol of the Tao on his chest, having studied and reflected sufficiently on that philosophy to have found strength and communion with it. I have friends of all faiths and friends who are atheists. I have still more friends who are an amalgamation of theologies and philosophies, who seek their own truths, and find peace in a number of venues defining themselves as spiritual rather than religious. The point is that we do not look at what is different about one another. We look at what is similar. We love and respect one another. We value each others' opinions and recognize what is true for all of us. We treat others as we would like to be treated. We love and cherish our families. We are kind and thoughtful of others. We love life. In our friendships and relationships, when we recognize the divinity inherent in each of us, we can transcend definitions of spirituality and see spirituality for what it truly is—a matter of the heart.

Though death reflection and study will certainly bring attention toward matters of spirit and we can certainly discuss these matters with others, we must remember that spirituality and faith are private matters. No one has the right to thrust dogma and ideology on you and you don't have the right to thrust yours onto others. What is far more important to focus on is to remember that we are all seeking peace with the knowledge of death and the pain that life sometimes brings. How we go about it might be different, but we are all seeking the same end. When it comes to matters of the heart, and spirituality is that, respect the tenderness of the matter. Respect each person's right and responsibility to find their own way in this journey of life. All that should matter are actions. If people are caring, kind, and respectful of others how can we justify insisting our beliefs are the only answer? You have not lived their life. Their journey is not yours. You have no idea what experiences have led them to where they are.

In discussing the subject of my book with strangers, as I often do, I have been surprised at how often I have been asked if it is a Christian book. I always tell them that I guess it could be, but I would not define it as such. I would not want to define my writing about something as universal as death by any one religion or to view it through any one lens. I try to explain my purpose gently. I remind them, Buddhists suffer loss and die, Muslims suffer loss and die, Jewish people suffer loss and die, atheists suffer loss and die—why would I restrict such an important and universal topic to one arena, to one group of people? I realize that most people are just trying to contextualize what I am saying into an arena in which they are comfortable, but more than ever we have to recognize the universality of the human experience. In death and grief, we can see more clearly than any other way the commonness of human existence. We can see the truth—that we are far more alike than different.

When discussing spirituality and divinity, it is important to differentiate here once again that I am not attempting to write about life after death, an area covered by most ideologies and religions. I have no idea what happens after the physical deaths we grieve. I am comfortable not knowing. I prefer to focus my energies on what happens during this life, how I respond to change, challenge, death and loss. What I do know is that how we respond to life and loss can and will determine the quality of our lives. I am writing not about life after death but about life after loss, about life with loss, and life with death.

We will each seek different avenues to bring us some peace with death and loss. For some that path will be religion, for some personal reflection and development, and for others science or education, for most it will be a balance of all of these. For each, it will be a private and personal matter. In order to nurture and foster our own journeys through this truth of loss and death, not only must we respect the journey of others, we must respect our path as well. We must give love and attention to our needs, both physical and spiritual. In respecting our spirits and their growth and expansion, we must seek out friendships and relationships with people who can respect the personal and private nature of life's journey, people who encourage our growth as individuals and celebrate our approach to life and living.

We all have some people in our lives who live an angry or fearful existence. We all know people who try to foist their beliefs on you as the only way to salvation. Sometimes it is a casual acquaintance, easy enough to deal with, but sometimes it is a close family member or friend. If it is a friend, we must ask ourselves, what are we doing with them?

With death and life's impermanence as your reminder you can begin to question yourself about people in your life who are not respectful and a joy to be with, why are you spending time with them? Life is too short to surround yourself with people who bring you down. True friends nurture our energy and uplift us and there is precious little time for the others. One thing that death reminds us of is this—our time is finite. Why would you waste the valuable time you have with someone who drains your energy and makes you feel bad? How is that serving you and allowing you to make the most of your personal journey?

It is one matter to consider friendships, or relationships that we choose, but family relationships are not quite as easy to step away from, and in most cases we probably shouldn't. Sometimes we are related to people who try to bring us down and we can't change that nor can we change them, but we can change our reaction to them. We don't have to allow ourselves to be brought down by even the closest relative (and you know the one I mean). We can do what we can for them, and then let go. We don't have to be mired in what they want of us. People can only hurt us if we let them.

We have to be the change we wish to see. Remember, most people are doing the best they can with the tools they have been given. They may not have any better tools. Maybe, if you add some new tools to your kit you can demonstrate a better way, maybe not, but you don't have to hurt for them. And negative behavior always comes from unresolved pain, from confusion about life and self. Their pain is their pain, their negativity is theirs, don't make it yours. Your state of being is up to you, you can choose to live in happiness and to live fully, the power to do this is yours and yours alone.

When it comes to personal development and spiritual growth what happens internally will be one thing, but what we manifest externally must be carefully considered. It is not our spiritual essence that we proclaim to the world, it is our expressions and actions that we present to the people we love and to the world around us. Considering our own deaths or the deaths of those we love can certainly cause us to consider carefully the content of our expressions and the consequences of our actions. Nurturing a gentler self can be the positive result of reflection on death and loss. Fostering and developing kindness and care for others and for ourselves is the reward for facing mortality. Embracing to the depth of our souls that we are all dying demonstrates the vulnerability of all life, the fragile nature of existence as we understand it best. By holding onto the death that waits within us we can see what is sacred, what is divine. We are. Life itself is.

Do your best to see the divine in everything around you, even the people who bring you down. See them for who they are, not what they do to you. Separate from them when you need to and do not hold onto anything that does not serve you, and emotional pain from someone else does not serve you. Remember, you cannot change people, but you can change your reaction to them. The only one you have to work with is you. You are your own work in progress. You will be amazed at how powerful and influential your own strong presence is in the world. Beyond that it is not your concern, let go. By fully loving yourself, honoring the spirituality and divinity inherent in you, you will draw to yourself others who are like you. You will find that you are the only company you really need and you will need to know yourself well for the tough road ahead. Life will be painful, and life will be beautiful and the spirit is in you to face it—head on.

We must not only embrace the promise of death and consequently seek to be at peace with matters of spirit and the unknown, we must also embrace the passion of life, the divine and sacred life we know now. As I have said, I do not know what happens spiritually after death, but I can tell you what happens spiritually while we live—we love. Love is the essence of spirit. As humans we tend to think we need so much, especially in America—consumers extraordinaire. In truth, there is very little we need and the Beatles had it right—all you need is love. Love yourself enough to respect your journey, to recognize your strength to face life in all its pain and pleasure. Love yourself enough to seek out loving and nurturing relationships. Love yourself enough to recognize that you are divine, that it is life itself that is divine.

CHAPTER 8

Hold Close and Let Go, and Know When to Do Which

With death and loss often in our thoughts we will notice inspiration and opportunities for reflection everywhere. We will find resources for the consideration of death and the transience of life all around us and they will lead us to reflect on times of loss and to contemplate the meaning of death to our lives. One such example happened to me recently while listening to Alanis Morissette, one of the most enlightened lyricists of our time. Ms. Morissette sings a unique and substantial song entitled, "Utopia." In it, she names all the qualities and characteristics we humans would have in her version of Utopia. You must listen to it, it is profound. The day after the death of our fifteen year old, wonderful dog, I was driving around doing mindless errands in order to be away from my home, where the absence of Willie was overwhelming. I had Ms. Morissette's CD playing and for the first time really heard the line in Utopia "we'd hold close and let go and know when to do which." The tears came as if from a faucet.

Willie had rather severe arthritis for the last two years of his life. He took medication and saw his vet regularly, but he struggled to get up and down. I knew he was not long for this earth.

I was very aware of the expected life span of a dog his size, though my husband would constantly say, "Willie could surprise us all, he could live to be twenty-five."

God bless him. He is optimistic and like I have learned that many men are about life's harsh realities. Though they may think about death and loss, they prefer not to talk about it directly. And hope does spring eternal.

I watched Willie diligently for the signs I knew would be coming, but as is with most animals, they can suffer in silence. I had felt that if his suffering was too much, we would end it for him and I would know when this time came. One Friday, I was sitting reading and looked up just in time to see Willie come tumbling down the stairs. He loved to sleep at the first landing where he could see all of us coming and going. He cried as he fell, and his legs would not get him back up. I ran right to him, trying to reassure him, just as he lost his urine, I knew this was bad. I grabbed the phone and called the vet, it was 5:45PM and though they were about to close they told me to bring him right away.

Just as I was wrapping him in a large towel to take him to the car, our twenty-four year old son, Elias, came in. I filled him in on what was happening and he drove us to the vet where we learned that Willie would not get up again. Willie was not crying, but I certainly was. I asked the vet to give us a few minutes alone with Willie and told him that we would be staying with Willie as he was put down. I asked Elias if he was alright with staying with Willie and me through this difficult choice. I explained that he did not need to, as I had done this before and could do it now, but he wanted to stay.

I got down to Willie's face and told him we were going to let him go, but that we would be right there with him and that after he was gone we would take his remains to Taos where we will always have a home. I went out and paid the front desk for his euthanasia and cremation so we would not be held up when we wanted to leave. The vet came back in and we were ready. I held Willie's face in my hands and kissed him and expressed my love, Elias stroked his back and held my shoulder, Willie looked into my eyes throughout and as quiet as a whisper he was gone with one final wag of his tail. I once again asked the vet to give us some time alone, which he graciously did. Elias and I cried and held each other and we held Willie, thanking him for his magnificent presence in our lives.

That weekend I made a special arrangement with a small table at the point on the landing of the stairs where he always laid and where his picture still sits today. Several months later, when we felt ready we buried his ashes in his own private garden, with a stone I created to announce his importance to our family.

I go through this entire loss story because so many of us can relate. Ms. Morissette's lyrics got me to thinking that when it comes to pets, we are better at holding close and letting go. Especially the letting go, because though we do this with heavy hearts we often choose when to let them go, when to end their suffering. We cherish these wonderful creatures. We gratefully accept their unconditional love. We mourn losing them terribly, but we do know what their life span will be when they enter our lives. Pets are magnificent gifts we allow into our lives. Though we hurt tremendously when we lose them, we are often better able to cope with this loss than some others because we seldom have regrets with our pets. Most of us just love and care for our pets all of their lives. We don't get caught up wishing we had said we loved them one more time. We don't suffer from the guilt of an unkind word or deed to the pets. We often treat our pets better than we treat each other.

I find inspiration and wisdom in many sources, particularly in books and songs as both an avid reader and a total music fan. I appreciate the songwriters for being the poets they are, and find myself ever grateful for their abilities to transform common ideas and experiences into relatable words and melodies. As I reflected more on Ms. Morissette's profound line that had jumped out at me upon Willie's death, I realized that it was about so much more than death.

Death was just the beginning of the lesson, as is often the case. As I reflected, I began to see clearly that we must hold close to and let go of everything of importance in our lives. The first example that springs to mind is children, most of us realize that we must learn to hold close to and then let go of them. We have to hold them with open arms, they will always be our children, but they do have their own journeys to make. They can settle and be nurtured by us at anytime, but then they must fly away to return once more. Though many of us recognize this necessity to hold lightly to our children, it is not always so clear with our other significant relationships. We should also hold close to and let go of our lovers, our partners, our spouses (hopefully for you this is all the same person). Though we have to come together to be one, we must stand apart as well. We cannot choke them into submission, they too must be held with open arms. Smothering someone is not loving them. It is attempting to control them. In order to grow your love you must both be free to expand as individuals, to explore yourself, your thoughts, your ambitions and ideas. This is hard to do from a choke hold.

The old saying that if you love someone, set them free, if they are yours they will return, if not, they were not yours at all—rings true. This is hard to accept when we are sure we cannot live without someone, but the truth is one day we will have to live without them, or they without us. Keeping this in the forefront of your mind allows a bit more freedom with that holding tendency. Ultimately, it is out of your hands. In fact, it is out of your hands right now. Recognize that and give one another the space we need as individuals. It is a beautiful thing to watch someone grow and expand him or herself, to find his or her bliss. It is even more beautiful to come together to share the new directions and experiences you both are having. You can't do this if you are too enmeshed.

It is not just in relationships with people and pets that we must hold close and let go. We have to hold close and let go of all of our experiences good and bad. There is nothing wrong in dwelling on your pain at times, as long as you also dwell on your pleasures and blessings at least as much. Times of pain have to be held close and fully experienced, that is the nature of life, everybody hurts sometimes. But recall the second part of Ms. Morissette's sage line—let go and know when to do which. It will take constant reflection on this line to learn when to do the letting go and when to do the holding on and for each of us this will be an action uniquely ours. This concept of holding close and letting go is in you to understand and decide how to act upon, just knowing you must do both is enough to start with.

It may feel easier to let go of painful times, but it is just as important to know that the great highs will pass as well, each moment has to be let go of as there is a new one waiting. People who seek to hold onto the high times are the very people who often turn to artificial means to find them: alcohol, drugs, food, or whatever the "feel good" mechanism is. It never really brings the moment back. Just as the memory of painful times can bring us back to pain, so can the memory of joyful moments bring us back to joy. Know when to do which, know when to cherish your joys and when to revisit sorrow, and then move on. New moments await and you can't experience them when you are tied to moments from your past.

Living in your moments is an ongoing practice in holding close and letting go. Each moment will pass, each action you undertake will end, each sensation will fade, in fact change is the only constant. We have to hold close and let go of every moment that comes. There are times when these matters feel in our own control, when we feel we are able to hold on to situations and relationships, but that is an illusion.

My sister Mindy lives in Los Alamos, New Mexico where a forest fire recently devastated the community, rocking their sense of security and forever altering their perspective on the illusive nature of safety. During the fires as we watched the news unfold, we kept hearing reports that their street had been heavily impacted by the fire. We were all certain their home had been lost. It was not, but it has permanently changed her sense of security, the sense that this can't happen here. I recall talking to my sister after she was able to return to the home she had been evacuated from for nearly two weeks, a home she has lived in for nearly two decades.

She said, "It's strange to return to your home and no longer feel safe there."

I remember saying to her, "When you realize you never were, you'll be fine."

This may not have helped, in fact I will admit it sounds harsh, but I believe it. It is much like being asked to face a fatal diagnosis to be evacuated from your home in this way. One minute everything feels fine, you are cleaning the bathrooms, and the next fire marshals are shouting from loudspeakers that you must evacuate. Life can and does turn on a dime.

Living with a sense of the nature of life and death places this illusion of safety in its proper perspective. It is an illusion, death is right there waiting, it happens every day to thousands upon thousands of people. People lose homes every day, people lose their lives every day. Death teaches us that. Everything is temporary, nothing is in our control except our own response to matters. We can hold close, but we will be asked to let go over and over again.

We can hold close to our loved ones, we can hold close to the treasures and momentos of our lives, to our homes and the belongings in them, but one day we will have to let them all go. It is said in flippant ways over and over, "you can't take it with you." We barely pay attention to this anymore. But it's true. You can't take anything with you. What is more, when you face loss it is never the things that matter, it is the people, their presence, their smile, their love. Anyone of us who has lost someone we treasure would trade all of our possessions for one more moment with them. Why not realize this now? It will help us to let go emotionally of those things that don't really matter so much, and by things I mean things—material possessions—they are nothing, keep them in their proper perspective.

I had a terrific grandmother who would remark gaily when we broke something, "Oh well, if we never broke anything we would never get anything new!"

You really don't want to be remembered for clinging to your possessions. They are just temporary anyway, just like we are. Hold close and let go and know when to do which. Think on this line. Reflect on its many meanings and its relevance in our lives. And thank you Ms. Morissette for the reminder.

CHAPTER 9

A Friend Like No Other

This book could not have happened without the presence in my life of a wonderful and uniquely luminous soul. While examining and exploring death's promise and life's passion I met a kindred spirit, a fantastic, life-altering meeting of souls that has had far greater impact than I could ever have foreseen.

I met Carla in a Sociology of Death class. We sat far across the room from each other, but both being "returning students," i.e. older students, we noticed one another, quickly noting our similarities. As is often the case with returning students, we sat in the front, participated often, and embraced learning with enthusiasm. The death class was particularly an area of interest for both of us and soon we were meeting up after class and sharing our lunches on the grass-covered hills of the campus. Carla and I quickly formed a strong friendship, kindred spirits in all things that mattered to us. We were very close in age, had each been married for around twenty years to men we were passionate about, had kids of similar ages, both of us were strong feminists and both were delighted to be in school, changing the direction of our lives with education.

Carla was the most alive and effervescent person that I had ever met. Her life had been somewhat unconventional, being a part of a family band, at times home schooled. Having never graduated from high school, Carla had gone back for her G.E.D., her associate's degree, and was now completing her bachelor's degree. Carla had a very strong bond to her family of origin, loving and lively people who gave her a unique and beautiful perspective of life and its joys. Her bond to her own nuclear family was even stronger. Like me, she was crazy about her husband. Both of us had married at eighteen, something that as feminists we almost felt compelled to apologize for. How could we be soccer moms, committed to our spouses since our youth and still carry the banner for women's rights and recognition? We knew our hearts though, and were strong enough in character to have allowed ourselves to be led by them while still prizing our intellects and independence. We had mates who loved that about us—we had it all.

Carla's father had died not too long before we met, so the death class brought out all that she had been through with that loss, and we often discussed its impact on her life. Her father had been part Native American and had been exploring that part of his heritage. She and her only sibling, a sister to whom she was very close, had continued this exploration. I recall one of her colorful stories of making medicine bags with her sister. Carla said that when she explained to her dad what they had made, he reached up to his chest and pulled out a chunk of hair and handed it to her for her medicine bag. I was so struck by this gesture of closeness and intimacy, it was so powerful and moving. The gesture and its meaning held such significance for her as she had to face his very sudden death.

Death and the relevance to Carla's and my lives was often our main subject of conversation. I had yet to face some of the bigger deaths that would soon come, but I knew loss was coming, and I felt compelled to study, evaluate, and embrace it. We both felt that the only way to live in death's shadow was fully and completely, seizing every moment as though it was the last. Death study had merely reinforced what we already understood and further solidified our commitment to lives of passion.

Carla and I had formed an amazing bond in a very short time, however one completely independent of our families. Our time together had been uniquely ours, I think she met one or both of my kids at a lunch at my house, but her family had all been at school or work when I had been to hers. Our families certainly knew of our friendship with one another, but we each devoted a lot of time to our growing families and respected the time each other needed for that. Further, each of us had husbands who were our best friends and we each loved spending as much time as possible with them. Carla and I knew that whatever time we had for each other was perfect—it was a gift. Neither made demands on or had expectations of the other. We each enjoyed whatever was. We were the type of friends who did not need to see one another often or even communicate often to know the love remained and that we would have no trouble picking up right where we left off. This is the only type of friend I truly consider a friend, the rest are merely acquaintances.

I graduated the very semester we met, a year before Carla, and moved away from southern California that summer. Carla made me a beautiful hand beaded necklace as a graduation gift. It is full of unique and beautiful stones, rhythmic, yet random, exquisite in design. This gift from her hands and her heart is one of my greatest treasures. I moved to New Mexico and later Texas and enjoyed hearing from her two or three times a year for the next five years. Carla shared with me her joy at graduating the year following my move, then continued on for her Master's degree in Native American Studies. She had written her thesis on a particular aspect of a certain tribe, and being in New Mexico I searched high and low for a piece of jewelry from that tribe, finding just the right bracelet to send her in celebration of her achievement. Carla loved it and knew it was from my heart, well thought out, and especially significant in light of her area of study.

Though our contact was infrequent, it was powerful. My heart would leap when I saw a card in the mail from Carla or a message in my email, her communication was always such a joy, her light shined through everything she ever did or said. No matter how small my messages, she always knew just what my true meaning was and any responses from her were right on target. After the move to Texas had brought us some particularly difficult times professionally, Carla's card in response to my update of these matters had just the right mixture of humor and outrage.

Fortunately for me, our professional life moved us once again back to Southern California, but this time with a twist. We had built another home in New Mexico to divide our time between. I was elated to go back to the Southland. I would once again see my Carla! She was one of my first calls. We could hardly wait to see one another again.

My father had been diagnosed with metastatic prostate cancer about a year before our exodus from Texas. I had been in touch with Carla about it. This was the death I had always known would come first for me. She knew how I felt about my Daddy. We had both been Daddy's girls. Carla was, as always, right there for me through the diagnosis, the illness, and later the loss. We arranged to get together within two weeks of my return.

Carla was now teaching Sociology at a community college and she asked me if I would come speak to her classes about my particular area of study, the Social Science of Health and Medicine, as it was different from hers and she wanted her students to see some of the avenues available to them. I was glad to do it, so we met bright and early one day outside of her classroom. Carla was, as always, vivacious and excited about life. She was thrilled to see me—giving me the mother of all hugs as only she could. Carla had followed her dreams and thoroughly enjoyed what she was doing. Her students loved her and she them.

In introducing me to her students that day, Carla expounded on her respect and love for me. She was never afraid to express her feelings and enthusiasm. I felt like such a celebrity as I stood up to speak. She built me up so much, I was unsure if I would be able to live up to expectations. I spoke freely and without notes about my experiences with my studies and subsequent work, ultimately landing on the topic of death study. I spent much time on this subject, Carla contributing as well, as we both expounded on the relevance of death study and reflection. I shared with students my father's illness and what it was doing to my life. I shared how I found my lifetime of preparation and reflection on death invaluable in facing what was coming. I spoke to three of her classes that day and Carla and I had a great lunch together like old times. We were hardly able to leave one another after five hours shared.

Our lives continued as lives do, busy and filled with what was important to each of us. We saw one another each semester for the next two years, as I came to speak to classes regularly for her. Carla was very excited at one such visit as she and her husband were enjoying themselves immensely with Harleys they had recently bought. She came to my home for lunch one of these times, finally meeting my Lee for the first time. We had talked often of our lovers. We knew the glory of each other's loves. Lee thoroughly enjoyed her, as everyone must, and after six plus years of my knowing her, was brought into the fold of those who were blessed by Carla's presence.

My father died the day after Christmas 2002. I sent word out over the email to my friends far away. Flowers from Carla were the first to arrive to my mother's home in Colorado where I was staying to help with the business of death. I knew that Carla knew just what was going on for me. She sent regular messages and cards and she was the first friend I wanted to see when I returned to California. Her hug would heal like nothing else, and it did.

We met in early April 2003 at her campus where I once again spoke to her classes. I spent much more time on death study during these talks, sharing that my father had just died, sharing many of the experiences of that death with the students. Some of them had seen me in previous classes and had known of his illness. They could see for themselves the course his illness and death had followed and how I had lived true to my words using reflection and study to better prepare myself.

Students asked lots of questions that day, one student asked me if I was afraid to die. I thought for just a moment and then honestly replied, "No, I'm afraid to be the one left alive to grieve."

Carla agreed wholeheartedly and the class discussed this. One student suggested that I write a book, noting my enthusiasm for living despite pain and loss. I explained that I felt I had it figured out for myself, but that I did not feel at that point that I could suggest to others how to live. Many students stayed after class talking to both of us at length about this subject, it definitely struck a chord.

After our classes, Carla and I had a beautiful picnic on the grass of her campus. We talked and talked and talked. She excitedly told me about her application to teach full-time at a school up north and her anxiety about whether she would really want to do it. Carla also told me in the course of our long conversation that her father had come to see her the previous weekend, you recall he had died not too long before we met. She said he had come to see her a couple of times a year since about three years after his death, always in her sleep, but she knew he was there. I did not doubt her one bit.

Carla said he had sat beside her sort of surprised and said, "Oh, you're still here?!?"

She told me she had said, "Yeah, I'm still here."

He replied, "Well, not for long."

Carla was really charged up about this conversation, though not afraid. We discussed it for some time. I suggested perhaps he meant still here in southern California, particularly since she was in the process of considering something up north. She said no, she knew he meant here in this life.

Carla said, "I'm not worried though, he was so calm and matter of fact about it, I know there is nothing to be afraid of, he will be there, though my Mom has said , 'don't you get on that motorcycle'."

I told her, "Of course, you can't live in fear, you must live your life as fully as ever, after all, tomorrow is promised to no one." This was a subject we fearlessly tackled, joyfully investigated, and passionately embraced.

Our time together came to an end. We had spent three hours on the grass talking, laughing, marveling at the beautiful new ring her husband had given her for their 25th wedding anniversary, which they had celebrated with family just a few short weeks before in Las Vegas. As always, we left each other more energized and charged than when we had come together. Our friendship was like that, each giving spirit and energy, each basking in the light of one another's presence, each knowing the beauty that they shared without having to discuss it. Carla and I prized one another fully and completely for who the other person was.

We emailed throughout the spring. Once, in May, my husband had occasion to be at Carla's campus with students and she saw him across the grass, shouting to him and running up to him with open arms. She emailed me about her joy in seeing him, so handsome, across the quad. I emailed back that I was so jealous, not that she said he was handsome, everyone knows that, but that he saw her and was the recipient of her wondrous embrace. In the early summer, Carla emailed that she had been offered the position in Northern California, but was struggling with whether or not to do it and commute from her home and marriage. We discussed this a bit back and forth via email, and she ultimately decided to stay where she was. She knew her husband Wayne was too much a part of her for her to be apart from him for considerable portions of every month.

We e-chatted into the summer as we tried to form plans for Carla and her husband to visit us at our home in New Mexico. We had discussed Taos at length, it was just the type of place for her, and she knew it. One way or another we were going to make this happen. We set up some tentative dates to converge in Taos. Carla emailed me saying she would have to beg off the dates we had discussed as it looked like she, her mother, her sister, and her daughter were going on a girls' camping trip at that same time and she apologized profusely about changing plans.

Upon reading her email, I vividly recall thinking, "How fun! What a great trip that will be for her! She shouldn't be worried about any plans we had, she should go and have a wonderful time—how lucky those women are to be able to do this together—how lucky they will be to be with Carla."

I wanted her to have no guilt about anything to do with me, our friendship was bigger than that, I wanted her to go on her camping trip just knowing that I loved her and more than that—I knew everyone who knew her must love her as well. I stuck to my belief about expressing myself with care and forethought.

I wrote back to her "Don't give it a second thought. Go on your journey secure in the knowledge that you are loved by all who are blessed to know you."

It was the last thing I ever said to Carla.

On Friday, August 22, 2003 while riding home from getting ice cream cones with her precious husband, Carla's motorcycle was struck from behind by a drunk twenty-four year old man, killing her instantly. I received an email on Monday from a professor we had had in common forwarding a message from another professor about her death, he was going to be doing the eulogy for her services.

The message said something to the effect of "I thought I should pass on the news of Carla Olson's death this weekend..."

I remember looking at it and for a split second thinking, "this coming weekend? Oh no! I have to stop that!"

I went numb, I could not focus, could not sit still, could not think, could barely breathe. I called my Lee, crying inconsolably. I could not even think about how to get more answers, what had happened? After calming down a bit, I scanned the message further and saw a few more details and I called her husband Wayne, to whom I had never spoken. He was in such pain he could hardly talk, but he did.

He said to me, "You can't believe how much it hurts."

I could feel his pain, it was physical, spiritual, emotional, and of such a magnitude I could hardly fathom. Wayne told me that he had my number there as one he needed to call. He certainly knew of me, though he did not know me. He told me what had happened, when services were.

I can barely remember what all I might have said to Wayne during that call other than I recall telling him I knew how much she loved him, that she and I had talked of it often. I recalled what Carla had told me of her dad's visit when we had met in April, I reminded Wayne of this during this call. I knew that if she had shared this story with me, she would have discussed this with Wayne at length. He remembered it as well. I remember telling Wayne that she and I had talked about what this visit might have meant and Carla was not afraid. She was not afraid to die. He knew.

It was later in thc day as I careened around my house in a fog, calling my sister and mother, calling my treasured friend, Marcie, that I recalled my last message to her—"Go on your journey, secure in the knowledge that you are loved by all who are blessed to know you." I was rocked by what I had said, how I had worded it, it now sounded so final. What made me say it that way? Why did I use the word journey? In my grief, I looked up journey in the dictionary. It of course has two main definitions. One definition is to go on a trip, especially one over a long distance. The second means a passage from one stage to another. I'm intelligent, I knew this when I wrote the message, I remember choosing the word carefully. Her camping trip was not a long distance away, but knowing her as I did, she would not take mere trips, journeys are what she would take, growth opportunities, passages—that was why that word had been chosen.

Perhaps I am not merely intelligent, perhaps I am intuitive as well. I do know for certain that when I wrote her that message I did not think even once about the premonition she had had from her father. I never thought of that again until she died. She and I had agreed not to be fearful of such matters, we weren't. I did not and do not dwell on possibilities.

I still do not know what element of spirit, intellect, or intuition moved me to write what I did to Carla, but I do know it is one thing that has brought me some peace in the face of this most terrible, wrenching loss. When at her service people were invited to share a few words, I shared how Carla and I had discussed death often and bravely, how our friendship was one built on this very foundation. I shared her visit from her father and how I knew she was not afraid. Finally, I shared what my final message to Carla had been, adding that I trust she has gone on this journey in the same way. Of course the services were packed to overflowing, and each person who spoke saw the beautiful light that Carla was, she had graced each of us in such a way that we each felt special in her presence, felt like the luckiest person in the room for the warmth of her affection and the completeness of her attention. I had been right, she was loved by all who were blessed to know her.

At her funeral, I finally met her beautiful children, her precious Wayne, her magnificent mother, and her very treasured sister, Cheryl.

Her sister came up to me after the service and cried out with the same voice Carla had, "I have to talk to you—She *loved* you!!!!"

I said, "I know, I love her too."

I explained that I knew I had used the present tense and that was purposeful, because I would always love Carla. Cheryl said she remembered what I had written to Carla about their camping trip because Carla entered it into her travel journal and had read it to all of them as they began their special trip. Cheryl was wearing Carla's medicine bag, the one that held a bit of their father's chest hair.

I will miss Carla every day of my life. I cry every time I consider that I cannot see her again or read a funny email from her. I ache to be hugged by her warm and generous soul once more. How could I have lost the very person who shared so completely my passion for life and embraced fearlessly the promise of death? We got it, she and I. We were going to grow into crones together, helping each other with the losses that are bound to rack up. But fate is like this. We believe that we never know what will happen. However, when we hold death's promise close to us, we have to realize that actually we do—we just don't know when, how, or to whom it will happen first.

As more time has passed and I grapple with the magnitude of this loss, I have come to realize that I am more complete as a person for having known Carla. There is more to me than there would have been had I not known and loved her. I know that any time we shared is now a part of me. Any love Carla gave to me is now in me and will be for all of my life. I would not trade one second of the time I shared with her in order to not know the pain I now feel. Carla's bright and radiant soul shined on me and I grew because of it. She will be my friend all of my life, it does not matter that I cannot see her. The love does not end. I did not stop loving Carla when we were apart and I could not see her and I have not stopped loving her because she has died. I will love Carla for all of my days.

When speaking to a death studies class recently about my experiences and reflections I was asked how losing her was different from other losses I have had to face, like that of my father. The student asked how I could not feel such anger and hatred toward the man who had killed her.

I answered her in all honesty, as I answer any question put to me, "Because anger does not serve me and more importantly it does not serve Carla."

In truth, I probably have more anger toward cancer, the pain and anguish it has caused people I love before they died. I have spent no time at all in anger over her death, I have no ill feelings for the man who killed her—his pain has just begun. There is no need for me to live in any of the pain he has brought forward, that pain will be for him, his family and friends, to contend with and there will be a lifetime of it.

Carla's life was about love. It was lived in love and with the rich fullness that passionate living allows us. She would have been the first to forgive this man. Carla loved young people, spent her life working with them, guiding them. She worked often with young men like him who were troubled and in pain. The truth is that it does not matter how Carla died, and though it certainly matters to many of us that she died, it matters far more that she lived. Carla knew, as I know, we all die, but the only aspect of the journey that matters is that we have lived. Carla lived and she loved and we who were blessed to know her are better for it.

This loss is one of the most painful experiences of my life. Its very unexpectedness lent an air of the surreal to the experience. There was no warning, no way to prepare other than the way in which I prepare everyday of my life. I loved her fully, openly, and unabashedly with a genuine warmth and pleasure that souls such as ours had found one another. The wrenching of Carla from my life has felt like a tear in my very fiber, but my love for her has not changed.

We have all heard time and again the phrase, "Love hurts." That is an utter and total lie. Love does not hurt, loss hurts, and it is love that heals. It is the memory of the love we have received unconditionally and the knowledge of the love we have given freely and without expectations that will heal our wounds. It is love, its memory, its presence, its very essence that will lead us through times of pain and darkness. Love is the light.

CHAPTER 10

Living Passionately with the Promise

Let us return to the definitions I began this book with and review the concepts of promise and passion. They are not just words. Embracing the essence of death's promise and life's passion are a way of living. Death by itself is no more than an assurance. It need not be solely imbued with fear. Death itself can simply represent nature, what is and what can be expected. Life by itself could simply be nature as well, but we humans are able to consider this force we call life more fully. We can explore and reflect on death and know that death is simply on the flip side of the life coin. It is in embracing that truth that life can be lived with passion, with great enthusiasm, with strong emotion and feeling. Life and death, passion and promise—hold one, you hold the other.

I have shared with you many of my own experiences with loss and with death and my beliefs about what these types of experiences can bring to our lives. What may not have been clear, what I deliberately did not explain is that I lost my dog, my father, and my Carla all within the span of one year. This year put to the test everything I have ever believed about the promise of death and the passion of life. This year was the very epitome of loss, of grief, of heartache and of pain. But even with all that pain, I knew what I believe about death and its lessons rang true. I was able to experience more fully than ever before what my intentions in living passionately, communicating carefully, choosing wisely and loving completely could do for me in times of pain and grief. I may have *believed* death could guide me to living fully before, I *know* it now.

While the question as to whether there is life after death is a good one, it is one we cannot know the answer to. Perhaps the more salient fact that we can know, that we do know, is that there is death after life. Holding onto this truth without fear may be the most important truth we can hold. Knowing this to our very core can help us to live as fully as we are intended to live.

When I got to the end of my death studies class we were supposed to write a paper wrapping it all up, tying together the elements of our inquiry. Papers for this class were unlike those in any other, annotations and the like were not as relevant as demonstrating reflection of the study. I suspect there were no failures as papers, but merely differing levels of understanding. We had read volumes of books and articles, had done several experiments and field exercises, had listened to quite a few speakers and viewed many videos. I remember sitting at the computer with my notes, books, and articles spread around me and thinking, "Okay, now what?" And that is exactly what I wrote. I wrote a recap of that which we studied but kept reverberating back to the original question, now what? The answer, provided in my paper as well as here, was the same at the end of that class as it is any time you ask that question. It is very simple, yet extremely challenging to those of us socialized in the West with its fervent denial of death and predilection for placing humanity above other aspects of nature. Now live. That's it—live your life.

No matter what we face, no matter what challenges we encounter, no matter what pain or pleasure we experience, everything changes and we will find ourselves asking time and again, now what? Our task, our answer, is the always same—now live. That is our job here as humans to live our lives, to breathe in and out. That is all we have to do, that and die—everything else is choice. As long as we are here, we should choose to live passionately—with care, with intention, with love.

In his book *The Voice of Knowledge,* Don Miguel Ruiz discusses the truth that happiness comes from the love you give to others, not the love they give to you. In other words, happiness comes not from being loved but from loving. That being the case, we can see that it is in our hands to be happy. We can give love as freely as we choose and thereby, choose happiness. Even in the depths of the pain of loss, there is happiness in knowing you have loved that person fully and without conditions. Their time with you is now yours, it is part of you and who you are. Knowing you have given love, unconditional and undemanding, will bring you some peace in your pain. My husband likes to say that it is the height of the mountain that marks the depth of the valley. It is no wonder the loss of one we truly and fully love hurts so very deeply, we love them at the top of the peak. We will go to our valleys, we must in order to journey forward, but we have to climb again and find the joy at the top of the mountain.

Making ourselves strong in the face of death and loss should be the focus of our lives. Being prepared for loss is being prepared for life. It is the same thing. Live fully, love fully, be present in your present moments and you will weather your pain. The only tiny bit of grace that can be found in these moments of profound grief that are most surely coming our way will be the knowledge that we did not let moments slip by, that we expressed our hearts fully.

Death reflection, death study, and death awareness can bring us closer to preparedness for loss and closer to our essence as loving spirits in this physical plane. Please remember that being prepared does not mean loss does not hurt, loss hurts like hell, it is supposed to. When we love someone dearly, knowing we cannot see them again is a true tragedy. It's just that we need not compound our tragedies with the extra pain of the "what if"s, or "if only"s. Know that you have lived fully, loved fully, made choices that had to be made, but made them with love and the knowledge and understanding of loss. If you do this, you will not add salt to your wounds and agony to your pain. Further, living fully and fearlessly, loving completely and without expectation will make your life richer, more complete, and your moments of joy will be magnified and increased.

While we have explored many lessons that death and loss can teach us throughout this text, perhaps the most important lesson is this: We must learn to not let moments pass us by, for moments are really all we have. Through the embrace of life's temporary nature we can learn to cherish each moment, to live fully in those moments. When you accept to the depth of your soul that we are all in the process of dying, you accept the choice to live in the moment, which is all we ever have, the moment.

When you are living in your moments, most of them are beautiful. Simple things take on new meaning. In fact, they take on the only meaning. In the end it will not be the big events that made us happy it will have been the small things. Our greatest joys will come from simple pleasures like taking a warm bath, eating well prepared, flavor rich food, laughing with friends, holding a baby, holding your lover, or holding your children-no matter old they are. Simple moments are the sum of your life. If you live in the moments, you will not let them pass by without expression, without love, without awareness of their fleeting nature, without passion.

It will be a delicate dance to be in your moments but to keep an eye on the future. We all have responsibilities and the business of life to attend to, retirement and health insurance to think about, car payments to make, mortgages to deal with. But it is possible to do both, to forge ahead with faith while enjoying your now. Finding peace in yourself helps you find the solutions to the problems you face, but finding this peace and the journey you take to get there will be yours uniquely. We will each look to different avenues to take us where we want to go, but we should know it is in *us* to find.

One of my favorite quotes, which I have painted in huge letters on one of my walls is from Ralph Waldo Emerson, "What lies before us and what lies behind us are but small matters compared to what lies within us." Finding what lies within us should be the focal point of our lives. Embracing the inevitability of death and loss, the fleeting nature of every moment and every situation, should help us to find what really matters in our lives. Death and loss are a part of us, true, but so are joy and passion. Death and its lessons are not somewhere out there waiting for us. They have been in us since birth. It's a promise.

Recommended Reading

There are literally hundreds of books on the subjects listed below. These are just a few that have been a part of my exploration. Remember, it's all about the journey not the destination!
Happy reading—JBV

On Death and Loss

Tuesdays with Morrie by Mitch Albom

Who Dies by Stephen Levine

A Year to Live: How to Live This Year As If It Were Your Last by Stephen Levine

The Grief Recovery Handbook by John James and Frank Cherry

The Orphaned Adult: Understanding and Coping with Grief and Change After the Death of Our Parents by Eugene Levy

The Wheel of Death, A Collection of Writings from Zen Buddhist and Other Sources on Death—Rebirth—Dying edited by Philip Kapleau

The Tibetan Book of Living and Dying by Sogyal Rinpoche, et al.

No Death, No Fear by Thich Nhat Hanh

Necessary Losses: The Loves, Illusions, Dependencies, and Impossible Expectations That All of Us Have to Give Up in Order to Grow by Judith Viorst

On Living Fully

The Four Agreements by Don Miguel Ruiz

The Voice of Knowledge by Don Miguel Ruiz

Simple Abundance by Sarah Ban Breathnach

10 Secrets for Success and Inner Peace
by Dr. Wayne Dyer

Love: What Life is All About by Leo F. Buscaglia

Living, Loving, and Learning by Leo F. Buscaglia

Loving Each Other by Leo F. Buscaglia

On Western Cultural Heritage/Sociology

The Denial of Death by Ernest Becker

Western Attitudes toward DEATH from the Middle Ages to the Present by Philippe Aries

The Passion of the Western Mind: Understanding the Ideas That Have Shaped Our World View
by Richard Tarnas

The Un-TV and the 10MPH Car: Experiments in Personal Freedom and Everyday Life
by Bernard McGrane

Referenced Works

Albom, Mitch. *Tuesdays with Morrie.* New York: Doubleday, 1997.

Huxley, Aldous. *Brave New World.* New York: Harper Collins, 1932.

Morissette, Alanis. *"Utopia." Under Rug Swept.* Maverick Recording Company, 2002.

Ruiz, Don Miguel. *The Voice of Knowledge.* San Rafael: Amber-Allen, 2004